Sporting

Legends

of the South

by

GARRY ALLISON

Publication Coordinator
Editor - Layout - Design
Barry Snowden

Occasional Paper No. 55

Lethbridge Historical Society
A Chapter of the Historical Society of Alberta
P.O. Box 974
Lethbridge, Alberta, Canada T1J 4P4

Printed and bound in Canada by Graphcom Printers (2011) Ltd.

First Printing
November 2013

Library and Archives Canada Cataloguing in Publication

Allison, Garry, 1941-, author
        Sporting legends of the south / by Garry Allison
; publication coordinator, editor, layout, design, Barry Snowden.

(Occasional paper ; no. 55)
ISBN 978-0-9867063-2-5 (pbk.)

        1. Sports--Alberta--History. 2. Sports teams--Alberta--History.
3. Athletes--Alberta--History. 4. Alberta--History, Local.
I. Snowden, Barry L., editor II. Lethbridge Historical Society, issuing
body III. Title. IV. Series: Occasional paper (Lethbridge Historical
Society) no. ; 55

GV585.3.A4A46 2013   796.097123'4   C2013-906392-7

Contents

Acknowledgements

Certainly in a project covering so many facets of southern Alberta sports there are many people to thank, none more so than The Lethbridge Herald for allowing me to use the stories I wrote while at The Herald and the pictures to go with these pieces.

As well I have to thank the Lethbridge Historical Society for publishing this work, the Society's Publications Committee including Shiela McManus (Chair), Aimee Benoit, Joe Kadezabek, Belinda Crowson, Judy Robins (Society Treasurer) and, especially Barry Snowden for his untiring dedication in seeing this book through to its publication. And Barry and I both wish to acknowledge Carly Stewart's editorial advice and assistance and to thank him for it.

Along the way there was the support and assistance of the Galt Museum and Archives, people like Pearl Mandeville, Lynne Davis and Mary Allison, and of course all the people within the book who took time out of their lives to sit and talk to me about the sports of their day.

The Lethbridge Historical Society thanks Garry Allison for providing his manuscript as a donation for publication and wishes to acknowledge and commend his continuing efforts to record and preserve his collections of stories.

The Society also acknowledges the funding assistance provided through the Alberta Historical Resources Foundation for its ongoing publications program.

Sporting Legends - a proud history

How many of you have considered the fact Lethbridge is home to a world hockey championship team, a Canadian basketball dynasty and the classiest of sportsmen's banquets, likely in North America, and for certain in Canada?

As well southern Alberta is home to world champions and legends in many other sports. I have attempted to document some of their lives in this book. You'll also notice a section dedicated to Kainaii and Piikani athletes who have reached the pinnacle of their athletic dreams.

A sport still thriving in southern Alberta in 2013 is basketball, through the high schools, Lethbridge College and the University of Lethbridge. But in 1960-61 and through 1962-63 Lethbridge and southern Alberta were the dominant powers in Canadian senior basketball, through teams sponsored mainly by Stan Broder, and rightfully called the Chinooks.

Southern Alberta's leagues came together in the late 1950s to form the first edition of the Chinooks, with a virtual all-star team. As the years passed, great local players were supplemented by a select handful of American players, many of whom stayed to make their homes in Lethbridge.

As great as the Broder's Chinooks were, they never won a world championship. That sole distinction for Lethbridge is held by the Lethbridge Maple Leafs, a hockey club comprised of southern Albertans who won it all in 1951, defeating the finest Europe had to offer.

Virtually all of the Maple Leafs players have gone now, but their stories, as individuals, as a team, and of their trip to Europe is captured here. I was fortunate to interview most members of the team and sharing those little chats is even more important now they are gone.

Another "ice dynasty" was the Lethbridge Native Sons, many of whom went on to the National Hockey League. I grew up, as have many others, idolizing Sons like Earl Ingarfield, Vic Stasiuk, Aut Erickson, Steve Arisman, Doug Barkley and Guyle Fielder to name just a few. Most are still able to don the blades and leave many a young player wondering what happened as they fly past.

While the Sons were certainly great, we can't overlook the Lethbridge Sugar Kings, the Broncos and of late, the Hurricanes. The Sutter brothers, Ron Delorme, John Davidson, Bryan Trottier and many more have made their mark in Lethbridge hockey and in the NHL. Their stories are for another time. Today we deal with the "historic" past.

The annual Kinsmen Sportsmen's Dinner attracted the top names in sports to the city year in and year out for 20 years. These super-stars ranged from baseball, boxing, hockey, the NFL and CFL, to rodeo and an array of other sports. Sports super-stars, many of whom had to look on a map to search out Alberta, let alone Lethbridge, graced the Kinsmen's head table from 1954 to 1973. The brainchild of Don Pilling, Bus Murdoch and Kinsmen like Harold Brown and Don Wilson, the dinner attracted many of the true legends of sports, especially when you look back as much as 60 years later.

The Kinsmen, who contributed greatly to the Lethbridge sports scene, also honoured the top Lethbridge athlete and sportsman each year, an aspect of recognition which has disappeared from the city, except for induction into the Lethbridge sports hall of fame. This collection includes stories of rodeo greats, Herman Linder, Harold Mandeville, Malcolm Jones, and in the native section, the great Tom Three Persons and Kelvin Fox. Many more rodeo cowboys might have been included - but perhaps that is for another time.

The final story in the book is a favourite of mine and centres on one of my favourite subjects, boxing, through the Jack Dempsey-Tommy Gibbons fight in Shelby, Montana. You may wonder what Shelby is doing in this book. In 1923 it was a trading centre for much of rural southern Alberta and a number of southern Albertans figure into the story - one a 105-year-old charming lady. The event has a strong southern Alberta flavour.

The near absence of women in the content of this book calls for comment. Perhaps it is a reflection of the world of the day that women were not an up-front part of the sports scene in

Lethbridge - hockey, basketball and with the Kinsmen's Dinner. I recall when Carol Hadford (Gemer) was named the city's athlete of the year in 1964 and she was "allowed" to sit in the back bleachers of the Exhibition pavilion (the men-only Dinner's venue) until her award was announced. Certainly women have made their mark in sports, but until recent times they were only "allowed" to be in the back bleachers. Rodeo is one where many women excel, but to this day they have to fight for recognition in the sport.

Sadly, many of the people in this book are gone. Very few of the Chinooks remain and even fewer of the Maple Leafs, while the Kinsmen dinners are cherished, but fleeting, memories for a diminishing number of sports fans in southern Alberta. These teams, athletes and events have left their mark on our world of sports, in its truest sense and in one way or another I had a first-hand look at all of these phenomena. I hope these stories will help rekindle memories for some readers, and introduce others to the days when Lethbridge was a major city on Canada's and the world's sporting front.

The Chinooks

Basketball in the late 1950s and early 1960s was booming on a senior's basis, with Lethbridge having the Green Acres, Magrath the Zeniths, and Cardston, and of course Raymond having top-flite teams. Then someone, likely import Bob Hamilton, created a southern Alberta all-star team for a run at the provincial, and Canadian senior titles. This was followed by a boom!

With the best of these teams coming together a dynasty grew - supplemented by American imports. One of the first of these was a pseudo cousin, Jack Lilja, which of course gave me an "in" and a new passion - basketball.

The perfect size for a basketball guard, in the eyes of most fans of the day was 6-foot-2. At 5-foot-10, Jack Lilja fell short of that mark and he felt his height, or lack of it, was the reason he never got a shot at the National Basketball Association. Dolph Shayes, a former NBA player and coach, shared that sentiment during a visit to Lethbridge.

But Jack could dribble, pass and shoot - today they would be three-pointers - with the best. Hamilton brought Jack to Lethbridge as a point-guard for the new southern Alberta all-star team. As well, Jack met and married my Uncle Al Walton's daughter Beverly - and they came to live with us for a while, with their new daughter. Thus a real basketball fan was born. As an aside here, Al Walton was, for many years, head pro at the Lethbridge golf course.

Uncountable basketball fans look back with fond memories to the days of the 1950s and early 1960s when Lethbridge was the basketball capital of Canada.

Upon examination you find the real success of Lethbridge on the Dominion basketball scene was due in large part to coach Bob Hamilton. "Hammy," who had more antics – and more knowledge – than the likes of Bobby Knight, moulded some

Herald Photo
Jack Lilja, local basketball star of the 1950s

super teams and laid the groundwork for the dynasty that was cemented.

Hamilton is gone now, but for basketball buffs of his era his legend lives on. A large part of this story is Jack Lilja, who came from San Francisco to play basketball here - and work for Broder's, the team's sponsor.

Lilja, who now lives on the west coast, moved to Lethbridge from his San Francisco home during the 1950-51 basketball season and suited up with Lethbridge Green Acres. He was a high-scoring, fancy-dribbling guard with an amazing accuracy from the foul line and sparked teams from this area to four Canadian championships.

However, many thought of him as the perfect guard. With the Southern Alberta and Broder Chinooks, Lilja toured Brazil, the Philippines and Puerto Rico. In 1963 he played in the Pan American Games in Sao Paulo, Brazil and the world championships in Rio de Janeiro.

Upon his return with the Chinooks Jack retired from the game as a player, but in the 1970s he coached the University of Lethbridge Pronghorn women, which included most of his five daughters.

The Chinooks were regulars as well at the Las Vegas Stardust Invitational Tournament in the 1950s and reached the quarterfinals once, losing out to BYU, the former team of one of the Chinook stars, Tommy Karren.

Travel was nothing new to Lilja, as he spent his early career after high school touring with the California Mohawks in 1948. "We toured Canada, Alaska and U.S. centres with the Mohawks," Lilja said. "We left Oakland, by car, with six ball players for the tour – we were a white Globetrotters. It was rough, rough basketball. It was fun, but it got to be a drag. We got pretty tired of travelling in that car, averaging 50 games in a two-month period. But we did have some good fun, though."

Jack had 14 college offers to play ball coming out of high school, and after serving in the U.S. Army had offers from Tennessee and LSU. But by that time he was already in Lethbridge, an established family man, and playing for coach Dean Bennett.

Despite the many successes of the Chinooks and other teams he played with, Jack had one major regret – never playing in the Olympics. He just never seemed to be in the right place at the right time. Early in his career, while still an American citizen, he missed out on the Canadian team and later it seemed the Chinooks never managed to win a Canadian title during an Olympic year. Today, of course, the Olympic team is chosen from the top players in the nation, something Lilja certainly was in his day.

"As far as my most memorable moment, well, they'll never take our first Canadian championship away," Lilja said. The Chinooks won the championship in Ottawa in the fifth game of a five-game series against Ottawa Joe Fellars, the overwhelming pre-tournament favourite.

"Most of our team were southern Alberta kids, and it was the first year Harold Brown and Stan Broder got together – Dean Bennett was our coach. Al McCann covered the series on radio and Don McLean was there for The Herald. There was a big parade when we arrived home. Fans met us at the railway depot and we rode through the city in open cars – kids even got a day off from school."Other members of the team included Tommy Karren, Al and Larry West, Don Doram, Bob Bradley, Glen Ennis, Doug Terry, Art Kruger and Ray Stevenson.

Lilja's era was a time when basketball was king in this city, as a skill sport, peppered with a few laughs. One time in 1950, coach Bob Hamilton threw his ever-present towel on the court after one of his players missed an easy breakaway layup. Sitting on the bench next to coach Hamilton was Bus Murdoch, and he reached down to pick up the towel. What Murdoch didn't know was coach Hamilton also intended to kick the towel.

"I kicked my leg out and kicked ol' Bus right in the nose," the 72-year-old Hamilton said with a laugh when I talked with him in 1995, not too many months before his death. "Bus spent the rest of the season sitting at the other end of the bench."

Hammy's towel, you ask? It was his badge, his trademark. It was his, long before anyone heard of John Thompson of Georgetown or the infamous Jerry Tarkanian. Hamilton had more uses for his towel than Gracie Fields had for her kerchief.

Herald Photo

**Broder's Chinooks Coach
Bob "Hammy" Hamilton**

"Bob started carrying his towel way back at Medford High, a long time before he even went to Lethbridge," said Marietta, his wife of 42 years. So famous was Hamilton's towel, the ushers passed out paper towels with "Hamilton Court" printed on them during the University of California Davis Gym dedication two days after Bob's death, Dec. 7, 1995. It was a ceremony attended by former players, opposition coaches and fans, from across the United States, coming to honour Bob Hamilton's memory. Even referees attended, including the head of the association.

Hammy was loud, animated, excitable and lived and died with every play, offence or defence – and those are just a few of the ways former players, trainers and fans described Hamilton when he first coached in Lethbridge in 1949-50 and then from 1959 to 1963. Knowledgeable is another much-used descriptor.

At his death, at age 73, Hamilton was the second-oldest college-level coach in the United States, only a year behind Dick Baldwin of Birmingham College in New York. In 1995,

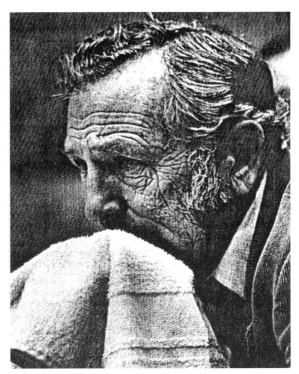

Herald Photo

Hammy was seldom without his towel

8

Hamilton was the guiding force behind the Yuba College 49ers in Maryville, California.

"I'm still at it, but there are times this year I've wondered why," Hamilton said with a laugh in '95. "It hasn't been that good a year. I've had two hip operations and have two new hips now. That has slowed me a little bit, but I can still get into it when I have too."

Hamilton travelled a 145 miles return trip from his home in Sacramento to the college. Because Yuba College is small, recruiting was tough. To add to the problem, you weren't allowed to recruit out of your own area. "But if someone up in Canada recommends a boy to me I can go after him," he said. "But he has to be recommended to me."

Above his bed was a huge photo of the 1962 Broder's team, a constant reminder of his days in Lethbridge despite his 47 years in coaching, 22 of them at the University of California. In fact he's a member of the Aggie Hall of Fame at the U of C.

Little did the native of Eugene, Oregon know when he served as a player-coach for the old Lethbridge Green Acres alongside the likes of Russ Fairbanks, Bus Murdoch, Kaye Jensen and Al Greenway, he was sewing seeds that would result in Canadian championship teams a decade later.

Soon players like Glen Michelson, Dave Stevens, Kaye Jensen, Don Tillotson, Doug Terry, George Hansen, Al Greenway and American import Jack Lilja were playing on the Green Acres and later the Lethbridge 77s in the early 1950s. In 1955-56, the team became known as the Southern Alberta Chinooks, a virtual all-star squad of area talent.

Players like Wes Rice, Tom Karren, Harry Blacker, Ty Alston, Glen Ennis, Logan Tait, Gord Fester, Don Doram, Larry West, Bob Bradley, Lloyd Harris and Lilja came and went off the Chinooks during their runs of four Canadian championships from 1959 through 1963. The first Canadian championship came in 1958-59 under

Karren Family Photo

**Magrath's Tom Karren,
a basketball star of the 1950s**

coach Dean Bennett with players like the West boys, Doram, Bradley, Karren, Lilja, Terry, Ennis, Ray Stevenson and Art Kruger aboard.

One of the most popular of those Chinooks was lanky Tommy Karren. The fulfilment of a goal is something few people achieve. Tom Karren of Magrath did fulfil one of his goals in sport, and it became one of his most memorable moments in basketball.

"With all the coaching and playing I've done it is difficult to single out one moment, but probably it would have to go back to the first time I ever played basketball in New York's Madison Square Garden," stated Karren, the former Lethbridge Community College coach. "It happened back in 1951-52, somewhere in there. Playing in Madison Square Garden was sort of a childhood dream of mine. It was a goal I sort of put into my life quite young. It was a dream, but I never thought it would come true. Somehow it panned out though, and I got there.

"I had always heard about Madison Square Garden on the radio as a kid, listening to Joe Louis fight, or hearing about the circus, etc. A friend of ours used to listen to the Louis fights with us. He was a boxer, and he always said he was going to fight in the Garden. Therefore, I always kept the Garden in my mind.

"I went to high school in Utah. We had a good team and won the state finals my senior year. That year I was named the most outstanding high school player in Utah, so a number of colleges were after me to play basketball for them. I signed to go to Logan, Utah.

"That summer Stan Watts and his family came up and spent some time on our farm. They told me I could have a future at Brigham Young University, and that the next year the Y was invited to a tournament in Madison Square Garden, and that if they did well they would be invited back.

"That New York tournament convinced me. I knew BYU was the place to go. The first year BYU won the National Invitational Tournament title, but, as it was my freshman year, I was not allowed to play on the varsity.

"The next season, my sophomore year, BYU was invited to the Christmas Tournament at Madison Square Garden. I had sprained my ankle a few weeks prior to the trip and had been riding the bench. I really didn't have any idea I'd play in a game. When we arrived at the Garden to play Niagara, coach Watts gave us a chalk talk, but didn't mention who the starters would be. After the team prayer we had another session, but he still didn't mention the starters. When captain Joe Ritchie asked, he was told that we'd hear when we got up there.

"Being on the bench I didn't expect to play, so I had kind of moved to the back of the group when the public address announcer began. The lights were dim and the crowd was a blur of faces. The first name he called out was mine. I didn't hardly know what to do. The PA guy had said go to the foul line, but I didn't hear him. I ran out to centre. They put a spotlight on the players coming out. And the guy kept taking the spotlight and moving it to the foul line hoping I'd follow. I didn't. Finally the coach hollered at me and told me to move. They all had a laugh at my expense. We won the game, and I played pretty fair.

"I was opposite Niagara's Larry Costello, who later played with the New York Knickerbockers and became a NBA coach, and I held him to 13 points. I fouled out in the final quarter and had eight points. I think we ended up about eighth."

Karren returned to Canada and starred for many years with Magrath Rockets, Southern Alberta Chinooks, Lethbridge Green Acres and Edmonton Townhallers. He helped the Chinooks to a Canadian championship before a leg injury cut his career.

Tommy turned to coaching when his career on the floor ended. He coached the Magrath Zeniths to provincial high school titles and went on to coach the LCC Kodiaks, winning the Alberta title every year he coached, and the 4-West title as well.

Tommy also played football and in 1952 played shortstop in the Big Six Baseball League. Shortly after his death his memory was honoured with the naming of the gym in Magrath High School, the Tom Karren Gymnasium.

Gord Fester, Logan Tait and Lloyd Harris were new to the Chinook squad in 1960-61, a season that held fond memories for Bob Hamilton,

especially the championship game. The game went to three overtimes with Al West on the foul line and Broder's trailing by two in the third session.

"Al hit his first shot but missed the second on purpose," said Hamilton. "We had a little play we'd worked on. Al had to miss perfectly so the ball bounced off the rim back out to him. He rebounded and handed off to Fester, I believe, and he went up and made the winning basket. I could hardly walk after that game – after all it went three overtimes."

Hamilton took over the Chinooks from Dean Bennett in 1959-60. As far as the personalities of the two coaches were concerned, it was a matter of being poles apart for fans and players. Hamilton was volatile, where Dean was "Mr Calm". Hamilton was in the tradition of Bobby Knight – a chair thrower at times, a towel waver, known to punch holes in walls, and he was loud. In one incident, Hammy was upset at the referees – believe it, it's true – and his players were up off the bench at courtside. The refs couldn't see the short Hamilton behind the players, so he jumped up on the bench and ran along it, waving his towel and hollering. Then the refs noticed him. But under the volatile exterior, Hamilton was a fun-loving personality with a sharp, knowledgeable and innovative basketball mind.

He and his Broder's didn't win his first year. They didn't even get out of the west. But they won in 1960-61, 1961-62 and 1962-63.

Asked to pick an all-star squad from the Broder's teams, Hamilton hesitated and then named Lloyd Harris at centre – but added he would also like Bob Bradley, whom he considered a great player. "We had good talent then, good people," Hamilton said. "By the time I came back up to Lethbridge, Lilja was a senior citizen, but he was still good, and a great passer. Logan Tait worked his fanny off for us and he was good on defence. Then there was Al West. Hey, Glen Ennis was a good one, I could tell you a lot of stories about Moose!"

He laughed as he recalled how Ennis once dribbled down the floor with his head down and went up under the basket for a jam. But he was right under the hoop and as he went up with the ball he rammed it into the underside of the rim and bent the hoop upwards.

Hamilton occasionally saw some of the old players after his retirement, like Fester, Harry

The 1961 Canadian Champion Broder's included back, from left, Harry Blacker, Don McClain, Ken Larson, Glen Ennis, Barry Forest, Bob Bradley, Gord Fester, Al West and Doug Terry. Front, from left, Bobby Broder, Lloyd Harris, Pete Vanderhilt, Stan Broder, Jack Lilja, Hal Brown, Bob Hamilton, Logan Tait and Bob Emery.

Blacker and one time Al West. "I ran into Lloyd Harris two or three years ago (1995) when I was out watching the senior golf tour in Sacramento," said Hamilton. "Harris had qualified to get into the tournament. I saw the name Harris and wondered if it was him. It was. I followed him around. He shot pretty well too, a 70, I think."

Bob Hamilton coached the Lethbridge Nationals, a Canadian team built around Broder's players like Gord Fester, Bob Inglis, Kenny Larson, Al West, Logan Tait, Harry Blacker and Jack Lilja at the 1962 Manila World Invitational Tournament. The Nationals went in seeded seventh. The Lethbridge Herald headline and story December 11th proclaimed a second-place finish for the team in the world-class event. They had five wins and one loss, behind the unbeaten Americans.

Later in the Pan Am Games in Brazil the Nationals finished sixth and at the Worlds, in the same country, they wound up fourth on the consolation side. "We did rather well considering the boys were all sick," said Hamilton. "I know they were sick because I was sick too."

Hamilton's basketball career in Canada, was more than world championship basketball games. He became part of the community, and even

became close to two of Lehbridge's top NHL stars. "We had a lot of fun in Lethbridge, my wife Marietta and I and our two-year-old daughter," said Hammy.

"When we first came up there we rented the Earl Ingarfield home and the next year the Vic Stasiuk home. They were both playing in the NHL and as we arrived they were leaving for the hockey season, so we were able to rent their houses. When we were heading back to the States they were returning home from hockey so it worked pretty well."

The Bob Hamilton era in Lethbridge resulted in three Canadian championships in four years and a Canadian National team based in the city. Hamilton's first year as coach saw the Broder's Chinooks lose to Alberni, B.C. and Alberni eventually lost to the Tillsonburg Livingstones, the team that went on to represent Canada in the Olympics. That was the only year in five that Broder's failed to win the Canadian title.

One of the key players on all those Hamilton-coached championship squads, as well as the 1958-1959 championship team under coach Dean Bennett, was Jack Lilja. He actually came through Lethbridge when Hamilton was coaching in the

11

city the first time, in 1949-50.

"Hamilton really knew the game," said Lilja. "He'd go a little goofy at times, as all basketball people from back then know. He knew the game though and he was well liked. I have nothing bad to say about the man."

Lilja said he and Hamilton came from similar coaching backgrounds in the United States and played very similar games. He said one thing Hamilton brought to Lethbridge was a different brand of game and coaching style for the Canadian-born players. Under Hamilton, Broder's was a fast-breaking team with speed, an array of shots including hooks, fade-away jumpers, lots of layups and some dunks off steals. It was also the era when there were no three-point shots. "I respected Bob as a coach and as a man," said Lilja.

During the final two years of Hamilton's tenure the focus of basketball switched from the Civic Centre to a new floor and the first glass backboards in the southern Alberta set up at the Exhibition Pavilion.

The portable floor could be laid in just a few hours and the backboards were lowered from the rafters in mere minutes. The floor was in sections.

The floor was used by more than the Broder's Chinooks teams. There was an international match with the U of L and Yugoslavia held in the Pavilion. However, when the Chinooks disappeared from the scene there was little need for the Pavilion floor. When the college and later southern Alberta high school basketball expanded their play, they turned to the Sportsplex.

The Rotary basketball tournament was also at the Pavilion, featuring the Cuban All-Stars.

Among the early southern Alberta basketball stars to play with, and for Hamilton, was Al Greenway. Hamilton coached Greenway, a stalwart of the Lethbridge Green Acres, in 1949-50.

"Hamilton both played and coached that first year he came up," the late Al Greenway recalled. "He stayed the one year and then went back to Oregon. Hamilton was very helpful, he taught me an awful lot about the game. He was as explosive

Herald Photo
Stan Broder, sponsor of the Broder's Chinooks

as hell though, even when he was on the bench. He was a good player. He was pretty quick, but really, he was awfully short to be playing basketball. He was a nice guy, but he was loud and volatile. Overall though, he was nice."

Greenway was still playing top-calibre basketball when Hamilton arrived back in Lethbridge. But big Al's career was winding down. Age and time away from work prompted Greenway to retire, which meant he missed the glory years of the Hamilton era. But like few others, he was playing at the very beginning.

Hamilton made his way back to southern Alberta in 1959-60 to take over the Broder Chinooks, a team that had won the Canadian championship the previous season. Doug Clark, one of the movers and shakers behind the scenes in basketball in Lethbridge for about 35 years, remembers Hamilton's return to the city with Broder's. In those days Clark and his buddy Bill Baker were among the scorekeepers for the Broder's' games.

"I've heard many stories of Hamilton, including the time he was diagramming things in the dressing room at half time," said Clark, who operated Doug's Sports and Doug's Travel until his death. "Hammy would point to players in the dressing room and say 'you should be here or you're supposed to be there' and to emphasize things he pounded the blackboard – and put his fist right through it. He was a very fiery guy.

"Hamilton was great for basketball here. He was a great promoter of the game. He's probably the best coach we ever had up here, but in saying that I don't want to belittle the others. But Hamilton was just that good." Clark added that one of the things in Hamilton's favour when he was coaching, was the fact Broder's Canning Co. was sponsoring the team and money was no object. If Hamilton needed personnel, Stan Broder would bring them in, no problem.

The late Don Pilling was Sports Editor of The Lethbridge Herald at the time of Hamilton's coaching stay in southern Alberta. It was a time when the rambunctious coach had his team on or near the top in Canada and in the world.

"Of all the guys I've met and dealt with, Bob

(Hamilton) was one of my favourites," said Pilling. "He was a good, all-around guy. I really enjoyed Bob. He was obviously held in high esteem down in California too."

Hamilton shared a love for music with Pilling and he enjoyed visiting the Pilling home and listening to recordings of the big bands and singers of that era. He'd never leave the Pilling home without his host playing Hammy's favourite song, from the "old" days – *Show Me the Way to Go Home*.

Perhaps the man who was closest to Bob Hamilton during his coaching days in Lethbridge was Peter Vanderhilt, longtime trainer and manager for southern Alberta basketball teams.

Peter, at age 79 in 1995, remembered Hamilton always got along well with his players. "He was a tough guy in the gym, but away from basketball he was a hell of a nice guy," said Vanderhilt. "He was always full of jokes and always laughing. His practices were tough, he'd work the boys hard. He was loud in the dressing room. I remember the time he put his fist right through the blackboard. He cut himself. I told him he'd have to fix it himself because I wasn't going to, and he laughed and said, 'Hey, I've got to show these guys I'm boss.' If he felt you weren't working hard enough he sure let you know he was mad. He took the game very seriously and you had better too if you were one of his players."

On the bench Hamilton concentrated on his own players, paying little attention to what the other team's individuals were doing, other than their overall game plan and defence, said Vanderhilt. He added that Hamilton was a good coach, knowing everything possible about the game, from A to Z. He knew what to expect from his players, what their limits were, and he expected them to reach those limits.

"If you were a good player and he thought you were doggin' it he'd sure let you know. But most of the times the players did their best and the coach realized that. He stressed plays, not just dribbling and shooting," said Pete. "He didn't have a complicated system. It was fairly simple, but it had to be followed. He pretty well knew how a player did, with rebounds and points, without checking the score sheet. And you can bet he worked on defence. The boys didn't play too much zone. Bob liked man-to-man better."

Pete started his training days in Raymond with

Pete Vanderhildt checks out an old basketball program

the vaunted Union Jacks, shortly after he came here from Holland about 1950. He started helping out, just wrapping a few ankles and ended up staying with them and then the Broder's teams for many years. "Those type of things just happen by accident," he said. "I was a school teacher in Holland and I had taken some athletic training courses."

Vanderhilt, who gave training lectures at the University of Lethbridge through the years, said players come to trust their trainer. After all, the trainer looks after them. Pete also became involved in hockey as a trainer, working with the Lethbridge Broncos at times, as well as other clubs. He was also a baseball umpire for many years.

One of Hamilton's first objectives in Lethbridge was to get some height on the Broder's squads. At that time Al West was about the biggest man, at 6-foot-3. So Hamilton went looking for height. Enter Bob Bradley, Lloyd Harris, Bob Inglis and a few other larger boys. "Hamilton would come up to me sometimes before a game and ask, 'how about Lloyd Harris, did you tape his ankles?' and I'd sometimes tell him they were double taped, because that's when he played his best," said Vanderhilt. "Bob would smile then because he knew that's when Harris would work his butt off."

Harris and Bradley didn't play on Hamilton's

Nationals because they were American. Jack Lilja however, another American import, played because he had taken out Canadian citizenship. Vanderhilt didn't travel on all the Broder's international trips, but he did go to South America for the worlds and to Hong Kong and Las Vegas for other tournaments. He and his brother were in business and he simply didn't want to take too much time off work. When he did travel his roommate was usually Stan Broder, the team owner. Hamilton always roomed alone.

Reluctantly - not wanting to offend any of the other players - Vanderhilt picked an all-star team from the players he worked with more than 30 years ago. Jack Lilja and Logan Tait were on his team. Both were smart players he said.

"For centre I'd take Al West. As far as an overall player, and being smart, he was the best. Though he was only 6-foot-3. Kenny Larson was one of the better forwards. He worked hard and had a good shot. Gordie Fester was a hell of a good shooter too and Harry Blacker was a good shooter. I liked his jump shot.

"Yes, those were good teams back then. They all played hard and they were all good. Hamilton never had to get them worked up, in fact he had to slow them down once in a while.

"I never heard from Bob after he left to go back to the States. He was into a different group down there and he'd be involved 100 per cent with them. You know, I haven't thought about those Broder's times for 30 years. Those were good days."

Al West and wife Jackie (Ririe – also a basketball family) have seven children, and all have played basketball at one level or another. Al came up through the sport, from high school to Canadian championship teams.

"High school basketball today is much different from when I played," said the former Raymond Comet star. "For one thing, the scores we had were half what they are now, possibly because of the jump shooters today. We used to have a fast break game, and yet the scores weren't as high as they are now. But in those days we jumped the ball at centre after every basket which slowed things down."

At 6-foot-3 West loomed large on the southern scene, but he was often dwarfed in the international games he played with the Broder's teams, where he starred in his later years. "There was one guy,

named Swede, who we played against in the Las Vegas Tournament and he was 7-foot-3. I looked him straight in the numbers," he said with a laugh.

West played in the Broder championship era, from 1959 through 1963 for coach Hamilton, culminating his career with the Pan American Games in Sao Paulo, Brazil. He also travelled across Canada with the team, to the Las Vegas Tournament, into other U.S. cities and Manila. The team was scheduled to play in Czechoslovakia, but the trip was cancelled due to unrest in Russia.

Broder's accomplished something few other non-NBA teams did in the 1950s and 1960s, they beat the Harlem Clowns – two straight nights in Lethbridge. When the Clowns fell behind in the second half they quit clowning and played real ball, but still couldn't catch the Chinooks.

Besides his brother Larry, Al fondly recalled some of the other key Broder's players of his era, like Lilja, Karren, Bob Bradley, Wes Rice, Lloyd Harris, Ken Larsen, Glen Ennis and Bob Inglis, and coaches Dean Bennett and Bob Hamilton.

One of the big tournaments Broder's was regularly invited to was the Thunderbird Classic in Las Vegas, featuring strong U.S. teams, sponsored by big industries. "These industrial teams were probably as good as some of the NBA teams then. We played an Akron, Ohio team once in Vegas and one of the players was Adrian Smith. He was in the NBA the next year and the following year was the MVP of the NBA All-Star game. Needless to say, Akron beat us."

Throughout his career West carried with great pride the fact he was first and foremost a Raymond basketball product. "With Raymond, it's pride, it's an attitude thing," West said. In his era Raymond was the team to beat and today, many decades later, teams still have to give that something extra which is always needed to beat a team from Raymond.

West and all these players had one thing in common – coach Bob Hamilton. Though stricken with cancer in August of 1995, Hamilton was still coaching basketball at Yuba College to within just a few days of his death Dec. 7th at age 73.

"He was still coaching right up to the end, but on Nov. 27 he came back from Yuba College and told me, 'I can't do it any more.' said Marietta, who was called Reet by her husband throughout their married life.

In June of 1995, Hamilton had been named to

14

the University of California Davis Hall of Fame with his induction scheduled for December 7th. "On the seventh, Bob just made up his mind he wasn't going," said Marietta. "He came home that day and said he wasn't going to go to the dedication. I tried to talk to him about it, but he looked me in the eye and said 'I'm not going.' He seemed to know something. Bob died that night. He had coached 48 years, almost to the very end."

Among his many achievements, he was the winningest coach in the history of UC Davis. He had also been told that he was to be inducted into the United States Junior College Hall of Fame. He didn't live to be around for those final two honours, dying two days short of the UC Davis ceremony. The event was attended by more than 100 of the former basketball players he coached during his 48-year career.

"My favourite explanation of Bob (Hamilton), is basketball was his first love and I was his first love . . . after basketball," said Marietta. "I accepted that, basketball was his life. Probably the fact that he touched so many lives is one of his most memorable achievements. Even though I knew that at the time, it has really come through now that he is gone."

Bob Hamilton was also a golf instructor and enjoyed playing, as well as watching the game. Ironically it was on an August golfing weekend with his wife that the terrible reality of the cancer first manifested itself.

He was a quality gardener as well. "Bob loved his garden and sharing his flowers with others, but the neighbours won't get flowers any more because I don't do gardening," Marietta said.

In going through her husband's papers after his death she discovered proof of the tranquil, sentimental side she always knew was part of her husband's makeup. "I found an envelope with 'Reet's Wedding' written on it. There was our wedding picture from the Eugene, Oregon Examiner. As well, there was one of those old Lethbridge Broder's brochures

Herald Photo
1979 photo of Logan Tait, 1960s player with the Broder's Chinooks

in another envelope. These were just some of his secret treasures."

A scholarship has been set up in Bob Hamilton's name at UC Davis, to go to a male or female basketball player. Marietta was among those setting up the criteria for the scholarship.

Coaching basketball players for 48 years is bound to leave a mark, but Bob Hamilton left more than a mark, he left behind thousands of friends. He was eulogized as an inspiration on and off the court, in the game he loved. Even though he was coaching Yuba College at the time of his death, Hammy's former University of California Davis Aggie team, with players who never played for him, wore a black patch with HAM printed on it for the remainder of their season.

Two days after Hamilton's death, the U of C Davis recreation hall was dedicated to his memory and named Hamilton Court. The dedication was set for halftime of an Aggie-Bakersfield game. Such was the respect for the late coach, both the Bakersfield and Aggie coaching staff agreed to the half-time ceremony, no matter how long it took. Aggie and Bakersfield players stood at attention during the close to 60-minute ceremony. Hammy's Yuba College team came for the event as well, and lined up on the floor, at attention.

"I wrote all the players a note and thanked them," said Marietta. "The dedication of the hall turned into a memorial service for Bob. Basketball players and coaches came from all over the U.S. It was quite an emotional evening. Bob's life crossed the paths of so many people. The Chancellor of the university was there and so was the university's gardener, both of them Bob's friends. Bob knew everyone."

One of the players Hammy knew and respected was Logan Tait. He had basketball in his genes. His mother, then Winnie Martin, was the original captain of the renowned Edmonton Grads basketball team. So it seemed somewhat appropriate Logan Tait's most memorable moments in sports are basketball oriented.

However, unlike most of

the championship Broder's players, it was a team from Vancouver that left the deepest mark on Logan's memory. Logan toiled for numerous basketball teams during his career including the Broder's teams of the early 1960s. But he goes back to 1959 for "the most exciting day you could ever imagine." The event will always be "clear as a bell" in his mind.

"It was my first international trip," Logan related. "I was playing with the Vancouver Eilers, the year we won the Canadian championship. We were playing in the world championships in Chile, divided into four mini-tournaments, with four teams each, in a round-robin. Out of that round-robin two teams in each division would move on to the finals, the rest onto the consolation side. Brazil, Russia and Mexico were in our 4-team division.

"We were playing Russia in the preliminary tournament. We were a non-seeded team. Russia wound up winning the overall tournament. Nobody beat them – except us. "We beat them by nine points, which we thought was what we needed to win by in order to win our division. It turned out later we needed to beat them by 13. Our fans loved the game against Russia. They were shouting C-A-N-A-D-A, C-A-N-A-D-A, all through the game.

"We had to take a victory march around the stadium right after the game. We had upset the strongest team in the world, but it worked out we didn't even make it into the finals.

"We had lost to Brazil in our section but had beaten Russia and Mexico. But, in the other games all the teams had beaten each other and all four wound up with the same 2-1 records. They went to points for and against, and had we beaten Russia by 13 we would have won. As it was we didn't even qualify for the finals and were moved on to the consolation side. Overall we won the consolation and wound up ninth. But really we were among the top three or four in the world, and we had beaten the number one team."

Logan, born in Vancouver but a Lethbridge resident since 1960 when he came here to play for Broder's, had many great moments in various sports. In basketball he played with Broder's Canadian championship squad in 1960-61, 1961-62, and 1962-63.

He also played in the Pan Am Games in Chicago, as a member of the Tillsonberg team in 1959. He has travelled to the Philippines, Brazil and Las Vegas for basketball tournaments.

Logan was on Canadian junior and senior championship basketball teams and had been on a Canadian champion junior soccer team, and has won the Canadian senior racquetball championship. "There have been lots of wins and lots of losses through the years," Logan stated. "But the highlight of my entire career is that tournament in Chile, my first time away, when I played as well as I have ever played in my life."

One of Bob Hamilton's long-time friends was Bus Murdoch, who lived in Santa Barbara, California. Bus was Lethbridge recreation director from 1948 to 1953, and with Glen Hamilton was instrumental in luring Bob Hamilton from Eugene, Oregon to Lethbridge as a player-coach in the old International League.

"Bob did a tremendous amount to revolutionize basketball in southern Alberta," Bus said. "He was extremely dedicated and took the game quite seriously. Bob had a keen insight for the game. The best word to describe him is dedication."

Murdoch recalled an International League game in Browning, Montana where Lethbridge lost. Among the forwards were Murdoch and Wren Mitchell of Raymond. "We were having a terrible game and when we lost Hammy was so mad that he came into the dressing room and punched his fist through a metal locker. Wren and I started laughing and he became madder. It shows you how intense Bob was where basketball was concerned."

"Once at a press conference in a downtown coffee shop, a reporter asked Bob (Hamilton) where he was staying," said Murdoch. "He said, 'My gosh, I just stayed at Murdoch's and all I could see this morning were kids coming out of the woodwork.' That was Bob, he always had a lot of fun."

Murdoch, who had a young family of 10 at the time, was living at Fort Whoop-Up, a recreation complex where the Lethbridge College Barn and a two-storey brick house remain today. If buildings could talk . . . well the sports stories would fill volumes.

Murdoch had a vision of a major western fun centre, with the huge building and a stock car track just to the west of the barn.

There were dozens of players who stood out through the 1950s and 1960s, and certainly older basketball fans in southern Alberta will recall The

Bus Murdoch refurbished an old brick, two storey house, built in about 1903, which was a natural thing to do. But he also built a stock car track to the west of the house, and a huge barn-like building between the two, just off the north. The tiled roof on the building spelled out Fort-Whoop-Up, and the inside had a huge dance floor and meeting rooms. It was to be a community centre. It did play host to some of the city's biggest dances, with stars like The Limelighters, the Ink Spots, Buddy Knox and Bill Hayley and his Comets playing there. The building is now the LCC Barn.

Brad Murdoch

The stock car track roared with the likes of Ron Boyce, Roy Nelson and triple seven car of Alvin Bolokosky.

"Dad wanted to build a whole guest ranch complex," Bus' late son Brad said during his final visit home. "He had ideas for a golf course, a hotel and other attractions . . . But financing got in the way."

Spider, among the others.

Reed Erickson was a teacher and became principal at the Lethbridge Collegiate Institute, but in prior years he was one of the better basketball players this area has produced – as well as a novice mountain climber who earned the nickname "The Spider". Reed played his high school basketball in the tiny community of Stirling and went on to play for the University of Alberta, the Raymond Union Jacks and the Lethbridge Green Acres and 76s of the pre-Broder era.

"One of my best memories has to be my last high school game," Reed stated. "There we were, from a little joint like Stirling and we won the Alberta A boys' championship in 1942. We had to play the best two out of three against Cardston. In the final

Herald Photo
**The original Spiderman
Reed Erickson in 1979**

game, with six seconds left, I made a foul shot that ended up winning the title for us. The year before, our first year in the league, we didn't even win a single game. Then, the next year, we were provincial champions."

Erickson was known throughout his basketball days as Spider. He laughed as he recalled how he earned the nickname. "The term had nothing to do with basketball or sport," he laughingly recalled. "We were in Waterton, my brothers and a friend and I, and we climbed to the top of the Bears Hump. Incidentally, the night before at a dance we'd heard this guy referring to himself as a spider. But back to the mountain. We decided to climb down the front face, a real steep climb, and we got hung up. We couldn't move for quite a while. A large crowd gathered by Crandle Lodge. A fellow climbed up with a camera to get our picture and I hollered at him, 'hey, if you think that guy last night was a spider, you should see us' and the Spider nickname stuck."

Erickson, who also used to play baseball with George Yanosik's Reos, was part of a Lethbridge provincial championship basketball team as well. "I really don't recall right off if it was with the Green Acres or the 76s – we went by both names. We beat Edmonton for the title. We had guys on the team like Al Greenway, Walt Harris, Keith Merrill, Bob Lindsay and Glen Michelson to name some. You know, one of the most frustrating experiences was the year I played with the U of A and we played against Lethbridge when Jack Lilja was with them. It was my job to check him. If I played loose and sagged he'd hit from 30 feet. If I'd crowd him, he'd make his move and go around me. I think he wound up with 27 points.

"Then there were those old battles between Raymond and Magrath – it used to drive me crazy trying to keep track of opposing player Wes Rice (later with Broder's) and I think Dick Sabey had more elbows and knees than anyone I played against," Erickson said.

Any sport has to have key people behind the scenes in order to succeed and one of the unsung heroes in southern Alberta sports circles was Doug Clark. For umpteen dozen years Doug toiled behind the scenes, keeping senior men's basketball alive in southern Alberta. Doug was never a player, or a coach. "There are enough dummies doing that," he laughed. But he was the key to the sport for years, as a backer and organizer.

Lethbridge held a popular Christmas Tournament that existed solely because of Doug Clark's hard work and love for basketball. And the Chinook men's league was mainly his baby as well. The Christmas Tournament began in 1952, started by Bus Murdoch, Lee Wall and Wes Rice. But soon Doug was working behind the scenes with people like Steve Tollestrup and Lefty Esphpieter.

By 1963 Doug was on his own. Not only did he support the sport through organization – and cash – but he backed "Doug's", a senior team for 16 years, which made it the oldest independent basketball team in existence in this area. Doug even underwrote individual players' expenses at secondary educational institutions.

The Doug's squad captured the Chinook title on at least 12 occasions and represented this area six or seven times in Canadian senior men's championship competition.

One reason Doug was involved with basketball was his sons. For years his eldest son Dave toiled in the league and then number two son, Jimmy, joined The Doug's.

Doug had begun a record business in 1956, on a $100 down payment and $235 a month rent for the appliance, guitar and 78-record store. He fought off bankruptcy a few times, but once on his feet he got into the sports field by accident. Gary Bowie was athletics director and coach at the new Lethbridge Junior College and asked Doug to get him a horizontal bar. That was his first sports equipment sale, and he was in the sports business. In later years it combined with Doug's Travel. But business was always fun for Doug.

"I remember the night before Broder's left for Sao Paulo, Brazil for the world championships Harry Blacker and Kenny Larson were in the store, then on 5th Street, shooting baskets for dollar bills," Doug said. "Another time we replaced two

Herald Photo

A young Doug Clark

plate glass windows in the store in one day because we put a tennis ball through them. We used to play tennis and put someone in the window with a baseball glove to catch any errant balls – he missed twice in the same day."

"I remember the Christmas Tournament when Bill Baker was running the score clock – for the very first time – in a game involving the Winnipeg Blue Bombers basketball team, with guys like Bud Grant and Norm Fieldgate. With only a few seconds left in a one-point game, Bill forgot to stop the clock during a time out. Well, Fieldgate grabbed him and shook him and created quite a fuss. Bill never came back to run the clock again."

Doug remembers the 1971 Christmas Tournament, which still featured the infamous "back door," where teams still had a chance at the title after their loss. The Doug's lost their first game, 83-74 to the University of Lethbridge Pronghorns. "We had to come through the back door and played four games on the final day to win," said Doug. "We beat the LCC Kodiaks 82-65 to win the championship. That was really something. We had guys like Ev Nowlin, Lloyd Fairbanks, Jim Gladstone, Robin Fry, Roger Baldry, Don McClain and Randy Milner.

"Another very memorable game was in Winnipeg at the dominion finals when we had Orville Fisher from BYU with us. In the consolation game Don McClain was at the foul line and we were down by two points. Don talked to Orville, then went to the foul line and made the

> *Doug Clark could tell a million stories about basketball, but one I liked best was when he talked about a trip to Winnipeg for the Canadian championships with Doug's, and a few pickup players to bolster the team. Two of those pickups were seven-foot giants Arnie Frank and Bob Inglis. But they didn't really add that much to Doug's offensive efforts. To his final days Doug lamented about the time he took "14 feet of basketball player" to the Canadian championships and they away with only one point on the score sheet.*

first short. Don purposely missed the second, directing the rebound off the rim towards Orville, who went right back up with the ball for the win. That was the only game we ever won at the dominion finals."

The history of Doug's in the Christmas tournament was a sparkling one -- almost as sparkling as the turkey-laden buns Doug's wife Nola supplied to all those who gathered in the upper room of the Civic Sports Centre each year. Doug's won the tourney six times since 1964, more than any other team in the 25 year history of the tourney. During that winning period three members of the Doug's team won the tournament's most valuable player award, Robin Fry, Don McClain and Gordon Balog.

Doug's first team was in 1961 and included such well-known basketball names as Ev Nowlin, Al Greenway, Bill Pizzey, Knobby Dzuren and Jim Furlong. Since that time the list of "stars" who have toiled with Doug's is a long one, including the likes of Tom Sindlinger, Bob Babki, Logan Tait, Alex Dudas, Larry "Ox" Baker, Jim Gladstone, of course Dave and Jimmy Clark, Clark Sloan, Danny Court, Lauren Edlund, Curt Wolsey, Roger Baldry; and dozens more, including long-time coach Wes Rice.

Doug was president of the Alberta Amateur Basketball Association for 10 years in the 1960s and 1970s. Whenever basketball needed help, Doug Clark was there – and often, so was Wes Rice. Wes Rice of Magrath didn't miss playing many sports in his day. He did it all, from hunting and fishing, to baseball and basketball. He was even into the sport of rodeo as a promoter for a time.

But Wes was best known for his basketball prowess with the Magrath Rockets, Broder's and the Southern Alberta Chinooks. His accomplishments include playing in the Canadian senior men's championship, refereeing in the Canadian men's senior championships (three times), and coaching six times in the Canadian senior men's championships.

"I've had thousands of memorable moments, and I really don't know how to go about picking just one," Wes laughed. "Being picked up by the

Edmonton Townhallers (an arch rival of the Broder's team) when they went to the Canadian Olympic Finals was a thrill. We missed going to the Olympics by one point. The greatest moment probably came out of that experience. We were in Vancouver for the final game. The winner would go to the Olympics.

"It was the game of the 'big stall'. The score was only about 8-6 at the half. The Canadian Olympic committee came down and had us start the game all over again. Imagine the pressure. There we were starting all over again, knowing that the winner would be going to Australia. We didn't go.

"Also, there was the night I scored 55 points. That was a big game for me. I was in a neck-and-neck struggle with a guy on the Green Acres for the scoring title. I was with Magrath then, in the old International League. That game broke the scoring race open. It was nice playing with good passers – after all, I sure didn't get many points off rebounding.

"I played on an all-star team against the Cuban All-Stars, at the Exhibition grounds in the final

Photo Courtesy Galt Archives
Wes Rice, 1978

game of the Rotary Tournament, and that was a thrill. There were a lot of moments with Broder's, the Las Vegas tournaments, where we played against guys who went on to the NBA; also when we went to Ottawa and won the Canadian championship.

"It was a thrill for me to see my son Ron win the provincial 4A finals with the Zeniths. I wanted it so bad for him. I had played on the last 'A' team that won an Alberta title from Magrath – and you always want to see your kid do the same as yourself."

You can't relate the Broder's Chinooks story without dealing with the individuals, not only on the team but behind the scenes. A synonym for senior basketball had to be Doug Clark, despite the fact it was Bob Hamilton who took teams to the Dominion title.

No matter who was involved, the mid-1950s through the late 1960s were the golden era of basketball in this region. I'm glad I was there to see most of the games and got to know a lot of the players.

The Maple Leafs

As a young boy, aged eight to 10, my Grandad (Robert Allison) took me to the Native Sons and Maple Leafs hockey games at the old arena. Those were exciting times. My Grandad knew some of the Leafs - he was a bartender at the Lethbridge Hotel. My Dad (Andy) knew some as well - he was a bartender at the Dallas Hotel. I'm not implying all the Leafs frequented the hotel bars, but fact is both my Dad and Grandad knew the Leafs.

As a result I've known some of the Leafs for many decades.

The Sorokoski family used to have a small confectionary along 13th Street North. As as kid I bought candy from Karl. We would mess around like all kids, but when Karl was there, I behaved. You don't mess around in front of a hero.

During the only year I played Minor Hockey my coach was Hector Negrello. It didn't matter that I was the worst player on the team; it was Hec Negrello who was trying to teach me to skate. But some tasks are too great, even for heroes.

Through the years I've written a number of stories about the Maple Leafs, and many of the individual players, including the story leading up to the team's 50th anniversary in 2001. Lethbridge's Boys of Winter were finally being honoured. These boys had given this city world-wide fame in 1951, and in 2001, 50 years later they were gathering for one more grand night.

For me, as a fan, the 50th anniversary was a great show, but also somewhat of a sad one with so many of those Boys of Winter gone. It was a great evening, but there was one black mark that most everyone there noticed - the city's mayor didn't bother to show up.

In telling the story of the Maple Leafs, you have to look at the players, and that is what I have tried to do here. I hope you enjoy the play.

When the Maple Leafs won the world hockey championship in 1951, I was only 10. Those guys were my heroes. When my grandfather took me to see the Leafs and the old Native Sons play in the wooden confines of the noisy old Arena, I'd sit there, in my grandfather's season-ticket seats along the west end, and watch the likes of Hec Negrello, Billy Gibson, Nap Millroy, Whitey Rimstad, Don McLean or Karl Sorokoski ply their trade as few others ever did in this city.

Through the years I've written about one of the Leafs' great stars, Whitey Rimstad, and I always enjoyed his company years later at the horse races. I've listened to the countless jokes and stories of Billy Gibson, and Dick Gray and I argued many times about the pros and cons of being a rodeo cowboy and about the cattle industry. As well, Nap Milroy became a friend, and I came to know him as a grand 'ol man.

Certainly in my north side neighbourhood as a kid, I was aware as were many others, that Jack Sumner was "one of THE Leafs." Every time my father mentioned people like Jack, Nap, Mallie Hughes or the others, I knew they were Leafs. I came to know people like Don McLean and Bert Knibbs in later years, as well as Ken Branch - I holidayed with his brother Howard, twice, in then exotic New Orleans.

"The Lethbridge Maple Leafs date back to the 1930s, winning the Alberta senior title twice and competing in Allen Cup play. Those early teams included players like Kenny Stewart, Andy Young, Garth Busch, Pete Slobodian, Bob Kirkpatrick and Jake Milford, and were coached by Freddy Metcalf and managed by Herman Thole, from the Warner-Milk river area," said Nap Milroy.

The Leafs left the ice during the Second World War, when many players, including Nap, exchanged hockey uniforms for army togs.

"While in the service I played on an army team," said Nap, who first went to England as reinforcement for the Toronto Scottish. Nap had two brothers in the anti-tank forces.

He said the original Maple Leafs were assisted by the Sicks Lethbridge Brewery for a while in the 1930s, but they left during the war years.

"In 1946-1947 the Leafs re-formed, playing in the old Western Hockey League with Saskatoon, Regina, Edmonton and Calgary," said Nap. "When the league disbanded the Leafs held a try-out camp in 1949-1950, selected a team and played in what was called the Crowsnest League, with Coleman, Fort Macleod and Medicine Hat."

Maple Leaf Tom Woods writes on the Leafs'

web-site that the road to the championship really "all began in 1940 when Ed Bruchet organized the Lethbridge Native Sons. During the war years, the only hockey played in Lethbridge was at the midget and juvenile level. Several of the players on the Maple Leafs were graduates of the Native Sons - Billy Gibson, Don McLean, Bill Chandler, Rob McGregor, Shorty Malacko and me, Tom Wood."

They all played on Ed Bruchet teams. Other team members - Dick Gray, Hec Negrello, Mallie Hughes and Whitey Rimstad - played for the Maple Leafs during the late 1940s.

When Sick's Brewery ceased sponsorship of the Maple Leafs of Western Canada's 1948 Senior League, all the above players joined with other local players like Nap Milroy, Lou Siray and Bert Knibbs, writes Tom. Their idea was to play the odd exhibition game on a team organized by local sportsman Addie Donaldson (who didn't make the trip to Europe.)"

"It was kind of a scrambled up deal, not a firm league, and we also played against a couple of Calgary teams," said Nap. "In 1950 we won the provincial championship. We had beaten the teams in southern Alberta, starting with Coleman, which always had a good team. We won the provincials and then we beat out the Trail Smoke Eaters."

Beating Trail wasn't easy. The Leafs lost the first two games to Trail, without Negrello, playing on neutral ice at Kelowna. Winning the next two, the Leafs were down by two with three minutes to play in the championship game, but came back to tie things up, going on to win in overtime. Next came the Melville Millionaires. It took eight games to win the Western Canada Intermediate title, with one game ending in a tie. With the win, the Leafs earned the right to challenge for the world championship the following season.

"This was amateur hockey and there was no Canadian championship as such at the time," Nap said. "We were ranked as intermediates, but we were seniors. I was 28 when we went overseas."

Tom says everyone maintained local employment. Nobody was paid and "we played just for the love of the game, the fellowship and the occasional beer." writes Woods. He added that what happened from a point in 1949 to the world championship in 1951 was a remarkable story.

"The first major step along this incredible journey occurred in the spring of 1950 when we beat the Camrose Maroons for the Alberta championship. We then played the Trail Smoke Eaters. The next

hard-fought series was against the Melville Millionaires. It took us eight games before we finally prevailed, winning the Western Canada Championship."

Tommy felt no one on the team could have imagined the Leafs would be chosen to represent Canada in the 1951 World's Championship.

In those days there were only eight teams in the NHL but there were hundreds of amateur teams across Canada he pointed out.

"At that time, teams who thought they had a chance to represent Canada in the World's Championship would submit an application through the provincial association to the Canadian Amateur Hockey Association," writes Tom. "Harold Brandreth, who was President of the Alberta Amateur Hockey Association, submitted our team. I believe our chance of being selected was enhanced because the Edmonton Watertoo Mercuries had won the World's Championship in 1950 and other western teams like Trail and Kimberley had triumphed in previous years. In addition, teams from Eastern Canada were not as successful as western teams at previous world championships.

"In any event we were delighted to hear the good news. Here was a gang of 'play for fun' hockey players with no sponsor and no money to buy equipment that had been chosen to represent their country. Upon hearing the news, the citizens of Lethbridge immediately rallied around the team. Most of the companies with which the players were employed, agreed to pay the player's salaries while they were away."

Billy Gibson said the Leafs' journey into hockey history was engineered by Harold Brandeth, president of the AAHA and J.T. North, of High River, with the Canadian Amateur Hockey Association.

"They did an awful lot for us in securing our right to go. They were two fine gentlemen."

To help pay for the trip the Leafs set out to build a bank account of $10,000 to be kept home to pay the players' wives a small income while their husbands were away, said Nap. The money came from donations from fans and city businesses and the ever-generous City threw in the great sum of $500.

"I was working for the City in the Parks Department at the time, and I got a leave of absence - without pay," said Nap. "Near the end of the fundraising drive Tom Kirkham gave us quite a bit, about $760, to put us over the top. We were asked to raise $10,000 and it took quite a bit of effort."

"A funny thing about the whole European trip was we had no bank account," said Don McLean. "We used to pick up $390 at Great Falls every Saturday and Sunday playing exhibition games to help get the money for our European trip. Well, two nights before we left for Europe, Great Falls drubbed us 19-2; we just went down there and tied one on. The hockey people didn't want to send us after that, but we worked things out."

The Canadian Amateur Hockey Association paid the team's travel, hotel and meals, but not wages. World amateur hockey executive Bunny Ahearne set up the schedule of games and cities, and saw the players received a small amount of spending money each week from gate receipts. And, of course the team had to be properly equipped.

"The CAHA paid for all of our equipment which was ordered from the sporting goods department of Consumer's Hardware where I worked," said Tom Wood. "We designed the sweaters with 'Lethbridge' embroidered across a Maple Leaf."

The 1951 Maple Leafs were fully equipped, first-class, complete with a $119.50 discount from Consumer's Hardware, for – are you ready? $1,046.43 for everything. Tom Wood, who worked for Consumers, negotiated the package, and the discount. You could hardly equip a peewee player for the same amount today. Try to buy goaltenders' skates for $100 today. That's what Sorokoski and Mallie Hughes paid. A protective cup was $1.35, a support $1.50 and a sponge 40 cents; then came a 15 per cent discount. The Leafs wore Prolite skates – the best money could buy. You could have fully equipped the Maple Leaf starting five, skates and all, for the cost of a pair of top-line skates today. The teams' hockey pants cost $125.60 and the sweaters, with the Maple Leaf logo, were $113. Two dozen pairs of hockey socks were $62, two pairs of hockey gloves were $21.50. Goaltenders gloves were $36.50 for a pair, their pads $49. Elbow pads, 15 pairs of large ones, totalled $27.87.

"After a goal, Gibby liked to skate to centre ice and stand with hands on hips, showing off those big, expensive elbow pads," Nap said with a laugh.

Shin guards cost $34.73 for the entire team. Sticks, not on the bill, were about $24 a dozen in late 1950. Today, one top quality stick costs more than that. To save money, CCM supplied the Maple Leafs players with sticks, $15 apiece.

Some were left overseas with fans, others with Canadian players living in England. Imagine having wooden hockey sticks left after 62 games, with 15 sticks per player. The key to this longevity was that Hector Negrello was the only Leaf player with a slap shot, and then he only drew back about two feet. More than costs have changed in the past 60 years.

"It was still hard to imagine that this bunch of local boys were about to embark on a four month journey that would culminate at the World's Championship in Paris," writes Tom. "But there we were, assembled on the CP Rail platform in Lethbridge on December 17, 1950 saying good bye to family and friends, about to board a train for Halifax."

No, I didn't go to the Leafs' 40th anniversary of their world championship reunion. Although invited, I felt that I'd be an intruder at an event that was special to those who were part of the reason for the reunion, the world championship. I would be an outsider. I was a fan - a youngster who idolized those Leafs and I was content to remember them from afar, and let them celebrate their days of glory and to remember the joy they brought people of this city.

But you can bet I was there for their 50th. I knew it would be the last time the Leafs would gather and I felt everyone should be there as a tribute to these men. My Dad and Grandfather were gone, and too many of the Leafs were gone, and I knew that in a few years all the Leafs would fall, and they'd only remain as memories in this ever-aging boy who saw them play when they were the best in the world.

Within this look at the Leafs I've added a few interviews I did with some of the Leafs who passed away years before the 50th reunion.

At one time if you asked for "Mr. Sport" in Bow Island virtually every resident would have directed you to the Bert Knibbs Hardware Store. Bert played them all in his day - baseball, hockey (with the 1951 world champion Lethbridge Maple Leafs) and most of the other sports.

Bert grew up on a small farm outside Grassy Lake, one of 10 children - they had their own family baseball and hockey team and just as exciting, brother-sister boxing matches.

"It wasn't until I was 15 years of age that I had a decent pair of skates that weren't strapped to my shoes," Bert related. "Our hockey sticks were mended with jam cans and our baseball gloves were our bare hands. But I can remember my Dad telling us that 'whatever you do, do it well and with your very best effort'. It was that incentive that led me to my many memorable moments in sports."

Bert was part of the old Southern Alberta Baseball League, which included Burdett-Bow Island, Lethbridge Galt Miners, Medicine Hat Tigers, Lethbridge Reos, Picture Butte Indians and Wrentham Red Sox.

"Some of the other baseball players around at that time were Fred Onofrychuk, Hec Negrello, Jocko Tarnava, Mike Seaman, Bill Kucheran, Matt and Sonny Slavich, George and Clarence Yanosik, Johnny Klem, Ed Dorohoy, Ted Smith, fireballer Ted Malmberg, Floyd Gilles, Loggie Erickson, Ken and Romi Miller, Elmo Elyison, Shortie Collins, Herb and Joe Thacker, Bus Allen, Pat Knibbs, and many, many others. In 1948 we won the championship with the Burdett-Bow Island Combines and it was truly a thrill to beat those city boys.

"Certainly another thrill came in 1949 when I was with the Lethbridge Maple Leafs hockey club and we won the Western Canada intermediate championship in eight games. My playmakers were Nap Milroy and Lou Siray, but "Napper" got hurt in the seventh game and we were allowed to pick up a junior player to replace him - it turned out that junior was Guyle Fielder. We won that eighth 4-2 and our line got three of the four goals, quite a thrill."

In 1950 Bert married "the prettiest girl in Bow Island" on Friday, but that Sunday he suited up with the Combines against the Galt Miners in a doubleheader. "Harvey Kjeldgaard put up a $5 bill to anyone who hit a home run that Sunday. I still have that same $5 bill to prove my story - It was the first and last home run I hit in a long baseball career. The honeymoon started the next day - and that proved to be another thrill."

In 1950-51 Bert went with the Lethbridge Maple Leafs on their four-month hockey tour of Europe and eventually won the world amateur hockey championship in Paris. "Seven times in that series the winning club's flag was lowered in salute to the ice surface and seven times it was the Canadian flag,"

Herald Photo

Bert Knibbs in 1980 with his world hockey championship medal from 1951

Bert stated. "Receiving that gold medal for Canada still sends shivers up my spine when I think about it. The warm welcome we received upon arriving home, the huge parade and all of the festivities, are long remembered. Another memorable moment was in 1985 when the Maple Leaf hockey team was chosen for entry into the Sports Hall of Fame. We each received individual plaques to show off to our grandchildren."

While Bert cherished all the aforementioned events, what he cherished most came in 1977 when he received a letter from Ottawa asking him to be in the capital in September to receive a Canadian Lifestyle Award. The Lifestyle Award is given by the federal government to one person in each province who worked in his community through the health and fitness program to promote that lifestyle.

"I knew nothing about the award at the time, but I received an all-expense paid trip to Ottawa and we dined with the Queen during her official Canadian visit that year," Bert recalled. "The application had been submitted by fellow citizens in Bow Island, headed by Fred Mellen, Claude Bishop and Oliver Hodge. You can't print what they said about me!

"The thrill of being driven from the hotel to the Parliament buildings in a sleek, black limousine was just part of the entire picture. We accepted the gold Lifestyle Medallion and plaque from the Minister of Health and Fitness, Monique Begin, right in the Parliament buildings, when Parliament was recessed to witness the occasion. Those events and the dinner with the Queen, with 50 sports celebrities in attendance, were great."

Another thrill for Bert followed the receiving of his award when he stopped off at Maple Leaf Gardens in Toronto as a guest of Lanny McDonald. He watched the Buffalo Sabres beat the Toronto version of the Leafs 5-2. "The thrill of being asked into the Maple Leaf dressing room and meeting pros like Darryl Sittler, Mike Palmateer, Stan Weir, Borje Salming and Tiger Williams, finished off my greatest thrill in sports in fine fashion."

Bert and wife Maxine had five children, Judy Ann, Blaine, Robin, Carey and Kalvin.

For Don McLean, March 16-17, 2001 was a time of fun, fond memories, and perhaps a little sadness. Don, and the remaining members of the Lethbridge Maple Leafs, gathered to relive the glory of winning the world hockey championship in Paris a half century earlier.

There were stories, like a team ski trip in Switzerland, laughs, and memories of times like a game being stopped after the second period due to rain on the outdoor rink, all coming during the team's four-month tour of England and Europe. Those assembled there also paused to remember their teammates who had passed on.

"When I went overseas I had just started a new job and had two small kids," said Don, who retired in 1991 after 42 years as an Alberta Brewers Agent. "Syd Frier, my boss, said to me, `Donny you're going,' and that was sure kind of nice. He was instrumental in arranging things with the head office and my going on the trip. Then he told me I had to make sure I looked up his brother in England, which I certainly did."

Don McLean was born in Lethbridge's Galt Hospital in 1926. In April 2006 he and his Maple Leaf teammates were part of a huge summer-long sports display in the building, now the Sir Alexander Galt Museum and Archives. Don was used to such honours. Besides his World Championship and

LETHBRIDGE MAPLE LEAFS HOCKEY CLUB
Worlds Amateur Champions — Churchill Cup Winners
Members Alberta Sports Hall of Fame

TOP ROW: D. Flanigan, D. McLean, D. Gray - Coach, W. Rimstad, B. Gibson, S. Obodiac, T. Wood, H. Negrello - Captain, B. Flick.
MIDDLE ROW: M. Roth, J. Malacko, M. Hughes, B. Chandler, D. Vogan.
BOTTOM ROW: A. Milroy, K. Sorokoski, L. Siray, B. Knibbs.   INSET: K. Branch, R. McGregor, J. Sumner.

Winston Churchill Cup hockey medals earned in 1951, he and his Maple Leafs are enshrined in Alberta's Sports Hall of Fame. Don was he city's Sportsman of the Year, presented at the 1970 Kinsmen Sportsmen's Dinner, and is also in the Lethbridge Sports Hall of Fame, to which he was inducted in 1985.

Don was schooled at the old Westminster school, then Galbraith and Fleetwood when the family moved to the south side for one year, and then the LCI. Right after school he started work for Commercial Printers as an apprentice printer under Jimmy Walker, but after a year went to work for the CPR. He started as a caller and later clerking in the rail yard under Ed Bruchet.

Hockey took him to Nelson and Nanaimo for a time but in 1948 McLean came back home. He accompanied Bruchet and his Native Sons, as a guest, for their trip to the Memorial Cup Finals in Port Arthur and Toronto, with players like Bill Ramsden and Eddie Dorohoy. "I started playing hockey about 14, when midget hockey went up to age 16. I got the Andy Anderson Trophy as the MVP in midget hockey. Then I played with Ed (Bruchet) and the Native Sons until age 20."

Don played in the old Western League and tried out for Buffalo in the American League, with 150 other players, before taking up with the Lethbridge Maple Leafs in 1948-1949. That year they won the western Canadian championship and the right to go to the world championships.

He was working at the old Sicks Brewery when Steve Pederson, one of Lethbridge's great bowlers, was working as an Alberta Brewers Agent and took ill. Frier asked Don to come to work while Pederson was off, and McLean stayed 42 years.

After his hockey playing days, Don turned to coaching, in championship style. In 1960-1961 he guided the newly-regrouped Maple Leafs, under Julius Lister, to a league title with players like Tom and Fred Zasadny, Stan Maxwell, Billy Gibson

Garry Allison Photo
Don McLean and his medals

and Ron Yanosik. He also coached the Lethbridge Sugar Kings, under Syd Hall, to a championship season with players like Don Hall, Craig Simmons, Gary Paskuski, Gerry Carmichael, Roy Fox, Alex Kogler and Jerry LeGrandeur. One of Don's four daughters married LeGrandeur, now a judge.

"My grandson David (LeGrandeur) was part of the championship U of L Pronghorn team," said Don with pride. "I had one grandkid ask me to coach his team, but once on the ice with those kids whizzing around, I knew not to. It was over, but I sure enjoyed it all, I was quite fortunate.

It was March 17, 1951 when the Lethbridge Maple Leafs captured the world hockey championship with a 5-1 victory over Sweden in the Palais de Sport in Paris. Those Leafs of '51 gathered 50 years later to celebrate the momentous feat.

The Leafs were honoured with a centre-ice ceremony during a Lethbridge Hurricanes-Calgary Hitmen WHL contest on Friday, March 16, 2001. On Saturday the scene shifted to Exhibition Park and the third floor of the grandstand for a banquet and dance. There were 13 remaining Leafs at the time, and most were on hand for the big event, which celebrated the Leafs four-month tour of Europe and the winning of the world championship and Winston Churchill Cup in England.

It was March 17, 1951 and goaltender Karl Sorokoski's birthday. What better way to celebrate than winning a world hockey championship. That night the Lethbridge Maple Leafs skated onto the ice at the Palais des Sports in Paris, France and defeated Sweden 5-1 in front of 17,000 hockey fans.

The day the tournament began, March 10, forward Hector Negrello had celebrated his birthday.

Don McLean scored a pair of goals in the championship game, as did Mickey Roth, one of three eastern players who joined the Maple Leafs for the run to the championship. Negrello contributed a lone marker,

Photo Courtesy Galt Archives
Karl Sorokoski

along with an assist. Bill Flick and Dinny Flanagan also added helpers.

"I had celebrated many of Karl's birthdays with him, from growing up on the north side with him, but this one was special," said Nap Milroy, one of the 13 surviving members of the 21-man Maple Leafs. "I think that was the best bunch of hockey players Lethbridge ever put together, after all we won the world hockey championship and you can't get any better than that. I quit playing right after that, I never played again. We used to discuss this with the guys, and like I told them, after that win you can only go one way . . . down."

Members of the Maple Leafs of 1950-1951 included playing-coach Dick Gray, Don Vogan, Bill Chandler, Ken Branch, Robert McGregor, Hector Negrello, Tom Wood, Stan Obodiac, Jack Sumner, Billy Gibson, Whitey Rimstad, Lou Siray, Jim "Shorty" Malacko, Don McLean, Karl Sorokoski, Mallie Hughes, Bert Knibbs, Nap Milroy, Dinny Flanagan, Bill Flick and Mickey Roth. Team manager was Addie Donaldson, but he didn't make the trip to Europe.

The Leafs left on their world tour Dec. 17, 1950 and returned home April 18, 1951. They had been selected as the Canadian representative on April 15, 1950 by the Canadian Amateur Hockey Association, after winning the western Canadian intermediate hockey championship against the Melville Millionaires.

The Leafs' world tour began in England, unceremoniously with a couple of losses. But by the end of their four-month tour they had played 62 games, lost seven, tied four and won the rest, at one time putting together a 44-game streak without a loss. In the world championship tournament itself the Leafs beat Finland 11-1, Norway 8-0, England 17-1, United States 16-2, Switzerland 5-1 and Sweden 5-1.

The CAHA panicked after the Leafs lost a few of their opening games and by March 8 they had flown in Bill Flick, Dinny Flanagan and Mickey Roth, out of Stratford, Ontario, to join the team before the world tournament began.

"Ken Branch, Jack Sumner and Robert MacGregor were replaced by the three new players," said Nap, who centered a line with Knibbs and Siray on his wings. "The Lethbridge guys played quite a bit of the tour but were sent back home before the world championships. It was just one of those things you had no control over. The three eastern boys were good players though, and they fit right in with the team."

Billy Gibson said no one could have hand-picked three better guys. "They just fit in like a hand in a glove, they were three good guys," said Gibby. "They were good hockey players too. They were one-two-three in the Ontario Senior Hockey League."

He was not a southern Albertan. In fact he'd never even been in Lethbridge until the 50th anniversary weekend, but Dinny Flanagan is entrenched in Lethbridge's history, as a member of the world hockey champions, the Leafs of 1951.

"I have often thought about the three players we replaced, and how they must have felt," said Flanagan. "It certainly must have hurt, but we didn't think of it back then. Besides, we personally had no control over the situation; they were sending three players over, and we were chosen." Flanagan, as an Irishman somewhat proud of the fact the Maple Leafs won the world championship on St. Patrick's Day, 1951, said he sort of lost contact with his two former Ontario linemates, Bill Flick and Mickey Roth.

The anniversary weekend was the first time Flanagan had even ventured west. The closest he'd come before was St. Francis, Ontario, where he was part of a team involved in the Allan Cup finals. And we all know Ontario isn't part of the west. Flanagan and his linemates had been playing with the Kitchener Waterloo Dutchmen when called up to the Lethbridge Maple Leafs, a time when he was just one year out of junior hockey.

"It was right at the end of our schedule," he said. "They came and asked us if we wanted to be members of the Lethbridge Maple Leafs. We were heading to the U.S. for a pro tryout, but it didn't take us long to make up our minds. We opted for the trip overseas. I don't think we could have gone to a team which would have accepted three strangers like us right away like the Leafs did. They took us right in. They were good fellows, every one. Now, 50 years later, they are still the same. That was the key to the hockey team's success, the camaraderie. That, as much as anything, is why we won the world championship."

Flanagan, who lives in Stratford, home of the Shakespearean Festival, played senior hockey after his championship stint with the Leafs, with Stratford. The team made it to the Allan Cup finals, losing to St. Francis. But that wasn't the end of his hockey days. He left the sport when he joined the Stratford Fire Department in 1958, but became involved in Minor Hockey and then in junior hockey.

Four years prior to his trip to Lethbridge, he retired as the General Manager of the Stratford junior team, after 21 years at the helm. His junior team turned out many NHL stars, including Chris Pronger and Eddie Olychek. But it is safe to say his hockey highlight came in the Palais des Sports in Paris when he helped the Maple Leafs beat Sweden 5-1 to win the world hockey championship 50 years ago.

"Don (McLean) had called me to come here for the 25th anniversary, then the 40th, but at those times I chose not to come," said Flanagan, now a grandfather of eight. "But this was the 50th anniversary, something really special. This will be the last time, so I thought I better go to this one. I was surprised with the banquet, and this city. I just can't understand how people are so receptive and how they pour out their emotions to these players of 50 years ago. It's so nice. The evening was unbelievable. When we think of hockey we think of the world championship. You can always put your chest out because we won the world."

Hec Negrello, Billy Gibson and Don McLean were the number one line for the Leafs.

For Nap Milroy hockey was fun back in 1951. "I had fun all the time I played, right from day one," said Nap. "Hockey was my entire life . . . well, hockey and then baseball during the summertime." Milroy, known as Nap because his father liked Napoleon, played his last game of hockey in 1951 with the world champion Lethbridge Maple Leafs.

The Maple Leafs were the last of the Canadian teams to go on such an extensive tour, playing in 14 countries, including England, Scotland, Italy, Belgium, Holland, Switzerland, Sweden, and of course the world championships in Paris, France.

Nap's early hockey experiences paid off in 1951 during the Leafs' quest for world hockey supremacy. Milroy, born in the city Oct. 7, 1922, grew up in the

Garry Allison Photo
Nap Milroy

1st Avenue A and 18th Street North area, and learned to play hockey on open-air rinks. "I played in the first pee wee hockey we had in Lethbridge, indoors on the natural ice in the old arena. Ab Holt and Charlie Dawson were very insightful back then in starting pee wee hockey, along with Andy Anderson. We went on to win the Alberta Junior B championship, with Ab as coach and Gibby (Billy Gibson) as our stick boy. Charlie was the manager and players on that team included Hector (Negrello), Gibby's older brother Dave Gibson, Karl (Sorokoski), Teddy Baird, and I think maybe Sonny Slavich.

"I started playing on the outdoor rinks, like all kids in those days, in the wind, snow and cold. When we went overseas as the Maple Leafs we played outdoors a lot of the time, in sleet and snow and we even played in the rain. In one game we not only cleaned the ice between periods, but stopped every few minutes to clean the snow off the ice during the game. But that didn't bother us, we'd all done that earlier in our hockey lives."

During one rainy game the referee had to put thumbtacks in the puck so it would glide over the water-covered ice. Meanwhile, the players who weren't suited up could sit in the stands and keep relatively dry. Nap said one line usually sat out for most of the games, playing with 14 players. The Leafs stayed in pretty good hotels, out of the elements, during their trip, and Nap said the team was treated pretty well everywhere it went. The meals were also good. As well, they got along among themselves during the four-months abroad.

"It was like any other team, there were certain cliques, with the same guys together much of the time. But we got along well considering how long we were together.

"Tom Wood was a bit of a loner, and was always off on his own reading books. One time he missed the train because he was sitting there reading and didn't get on with us." Gibby said Tommy Wood was reading Roosevelt's biography and got so enthralled he missed the train. "He had to catch up to us at the next stop." He didn't catch up with the team until the second period of their next game.

Much of the trip was via train or bus, but

> *"The best athlete I played with was Hector (Negrello), in baseball or hockey. He just had that hustle, that knack to play well. In hockey he knew how to put the biscuit in the net and the same in ball. He was an all around athlete.*
>
> *"In fact, I think he was the best athlete in southern Alberta in the last century," Nap stated.*

occasionally the team boarded an old DC 3 for a flight.

The team had boarded the steamship Scythia for the seven-day voyage across the Atlantic. On the way over the team would often play shuffleboard and be joined by the four or five people from first class for bingo games, not rowdy parties. They came back on the Empress of France.

Milroy grew up in north Lethbridge and would hang out with Karl Sorokoski. Later, after he moved in from Coalhurst, Hec Negrello was also part of the group and they were good friends.

Sorokoski and Mallie Hughes were the goaltenders. They had to purchase their own equipment, just as the regular players did. The two goaltenders would alternate games on a regimented basis during the entire trip. They did their job well. In the six-team, six-game world championship tournament, the pair only allowed six goals, while the guys up front netted 62. Stan Obodiac led the way with 12 goals, Gibson and Dinny Flanagan had eight apiece, and Don McLean, Mickey Roth, Bill Flick and Bill Chandler had five each. Negrello scored four times, Whitey Rimstad three times, Dick Gray and Don Vogan twice and single markers came from Milroy, Wood and Bert Knibbs.

The toughest games were against the English teams, which included about 90 per cent Canadian players. It was like playing another Canadian team. In fact, the toughest tournament for our Maple Leafs was winning the Winston Churchill Cup in Wembley Stadium in London. The Leafs' very first game was an 8-6 loss to Nottingham, New Year's Day, 1951. "But we beat them when it mattered, for the Winston Churchill Cup," said Gibby.

Some of the tour games were against pretty feeble opposition, others against top clubs. Sometimes the Maple Leafs would be surprised because the fans were cheering for them. During a game in Munich it turned out some of the cheering fans were former German prisoners of war who had been incarcerated in the PoW camp in Lethbridge. Most of the PoWs from the huge mile-square Lethbridge camp enjoyed their stay in southern Alberta. They showed their feelings back home by cheering for the Maple Leafs. Another game included a group of Swiss yodellers.

Families of the players back home were receiving a small amount of money from the fund raised before the trip, but the players were getting even less, garnered from games on the tour. "There was some

money," said Nap. "We'd make a couple of pounds or so, but not very darn much."

For Nap it was a memorable trip, but most of all he cherishes winning the world championship. "After all, that's what we went for," said Nap, who worked for the city as parks foreman for 15 years before moving on to serve as this area's business representative, for 20 years, with the Canadian Union of Public Employees.

Nap was honoured at centre ice in the Lethbridge Sportsplex in January, 2011, the 60th anniversary of the Maple Leafs taking the world championship. Nap was one of very few Leafs remaining for the 60th anniversary.

In 1947-1948, the Lethbridge Maple Leafs were playing in the old Western Hockey League, but the league disbanded at season's end. For the 1949-1950 season, the Leafs regrouped under manager Addie Donaldson. "We'd practice at 10 p.m.," Don McLean remembered with a laugh.

Billy Gibson said the team was formed after a try-out camp, where some players who failed to make the final cut were still upset many decades later. The reason for the anger became evident when the Maple Leafs won the right to go to the world hockey championships, as the western Canadian champions, at the close of the 1950 season.

As the Leafs gathered to celebrate the 50th anniversary, many were missing off that team selected for the 1949-50 season, including: Whitey Rimstad, Karl Sorokoski, Dick Gray, Bill Chandler, Mallie Hughes, Stan Obodiac, Bert Knibbs and Hector Negrello. But their names were brought up in many a story by the remaining Leafs as tall tales whizzed past faster than slap shots - a plague that hadn't infiltrated the game in 1951. You'd hear Gibby tell how the beams in one hotel in Nottingham were so low he came close to giving himself a concussion banging his head a time or two.

"In one stretch we played 13 games in 14 nights, in Switzerland," he said. "We never slept in the same bed twice. I'm talking heavy duty packing and moving here."

The trip brought the Maple Leafs into contact with hockey players they hadn't played against before, and there were some surprising results. Gibby called Chick Zamick "likely the best amateur hockey player he ever saw." "He was from Winnipeg and was playing with Nottingham in England, in a pro league. He ended up becoming the mayor of Nottingham, besides being a good hockey player. Orville Martini, from Calgary, was playing in Italy and Stubby Mason of Winnipeg played goal for Wembley. Wembley was beating us 3-0 in the Churchill Cup and they were ridiculing us pretty good as the game wore on. But we ended up scoring four straight goals to beat them 4-3 and win the Winston Churchill Cup."

McLean said Leafs' playing coach Dick Gray always had four lines to work with, but only three lines would dress for a game, giving the others a chance to rest or recover from injuries. "Hector was out for a while with a shoulder or knee injury and (Bill) Flick broke his wrist after the world tournament," McLean said, adding however, "the Leafs were relatively injury free that winter."

All the emphasis wasn't on hockey. Gibson remembered playing in Falkirk, Scotland and seeing Johnny Easton and Roy Hopkins, former Lethbridge postal workers, during a get-together after the game. At the time Gibby was circling the ice during warm-up and kept hearing someone call his name. McLean told him to check it out, but Gibby thought someone had just bought a program for half a crown and was being smart. "I didn't know anyone in Scotland. But I finally went over to the boards when the guy hollered Gibby, and there was Roy Hopkins."

Nap ran into Jock Clark, the old Lethbridge Supina's soccer star in Scotland as well. Clark then came to the dressing room after the game and it was like old home week.

During a day off Gibson travelled into Ireland to visit his grandparents and McLean was thrilled with a trip he took to Scotland. "I got to see the 'wee hoose' where my mother was born, in Wishaw, outside Glasgow," he said.

Once the team was in Europe, language was rarely a concern, though they encountered some language barriers when trying to deal with referees during games, especially in Germany. McLean said the team's bus driver was fluent in English and loved the movies, cowboy star Hopalong Cassidy in particular.

"Fred Tramp was our interpreter in Germany," said Gibby. "He had been a sergeant with the gestapo during the war." While the Leafs toured Germany Gibby remembered seeing some of the destruction from the war still evident, with some streets consisting of lone walls and rubble, the result of Allied bombing only a few years earlier. But the very next year, back in Germany with the Edmonton Mercurys for the Olympic Games, Gibby said there wasn't any sign of ruin. The country had recovered that quickly.

The quest for a world hockey title ended prematurely for Jack Sumner, Bob McGregor and Ken Branch.

"It didn't bother me in the slightest," said Ken Branch, who had been in Europe a few years earlier during the Second World War as a mosquito fighter pilot, flying night missions with the 409 Squadron. "I was sent back home in February, but we had already played games in Scotland, England, Italy, Switzerland and Germany. The team did play one game in Paris while I was with them, but I didn't play. I refereed. Dick (Gray, the Leafs' playing-coach) didn't like that much. I was too honest. I'd call him and give him penalties."

Ken was 29 at the time, and got as much kick out of some of the fringe benefits of the tour as he did the games. On the flight over from England to the continent, in a small, propeller-driven plane arranged by the team's tour director Bunny Ahearne, Branch piloted the plane. He said the crew invited him up to the cockpit to look around and allowed him to sit in and fly the plane across the channel.

For him, the trip to Europe was really more than he expected from playing with the Leafs. "Even back then, it was felt Canada couldn't afford to be beaten and after some early losses it was decided to strengthen the team, and three eastern players were brought over. I never did meet the three until much later. It was explained to us they had to strengthen the team. It was unfortunate, but that's the way it was."

Bob Kirkpatrick, a longtime Leaf from earlier days, didn't make the trip and neither did team manager Addie Donaldson, who stayed home to manage the coal mine at Shaughnessy. Born in Lethbridge in 1922, Branch was also working at the Shaughnessy coal mine at the time, along with Lou Siray and Bert Knibbs.

Though Ken Branch wasn't part of the entire tour he agrees with something Whitey Rimstad said in later years, about the team playing one day and moving the next. "You never would get time to see your underwear fully dried before you were leaving a hotel," said Ken, who died in December 2005 at age 83. "We met a lot of Canadians over there, playing in different places. We played an Italian all-star team with nine Canadians and four Americans."

Ken, a left-winger, came home before the world tournament and returned into the Canadian Air Force. It was the start of the Korean War and times were tense. Ken remained in miltary service for the next 20 years, learning to fly the sleek Sabre jets and becoming a flying instructor before retiring in 1971.

For the Leafs, there was more to the tour of England and Europe than the quest for the world hockey championship. The ship, train, plane, bus and car trips left their mark, as did some of the experiences along the way, from meeting relatives and fans to the food and receptions abroad and back home. The cruise over on the Atlantic, on the Cunard White Star's Scythia, was a glass-smooth experience and the players got in some shuffleboard and a fine Christmas dinner.

"There were only 112 passengers on the ship going over, so the boat was a little empty," said Don McLean. "The water was so perfect we actually made up a whole day. We were on the ship for Christmas Dinner in 1950." Don kept the Christmas menu, listing dishes like chicken okra, poached salmon, roast sirloin and ribs, York ham, roast Norfolk turkey, Brussel sprouts, corn-on-the-cob, salads, plum pudding, Christmas cake and ice cream with a wafer.

In his sketchy diary of the trip, late Leaf goaltender, Karl Sorokoski, briefly mentioned the team leaving Halifax on Dec. 22 and the Scythia's arrival at the Tilsbury docks 25 miles from London Dec. 30. In the back of the book, Sorokoski listed his record, playing 29 games in goal, with 22 wins, four losses and a tie. He and fellow goalie Mallie Hughes both recorded two shutouts. The Leafs played their first game in Nottingham, England, a losing affair, 8-6, on New Year's day. It was the start of many days, before and after the world championship, in England, eating English meals.

Stan Obodiac was writing a weekly column for *The Lethbridge Herald* from a player's point of view about the trip and his last column detailed some of his best and worst experiences on the team's 30,000 mile excursion to 14 countries and playing in front of about 400,000 people during their 62 games, of which they won 51 and tied four.

The worst food and climate, he wrote, was in

Bill Barilko

"Max Bentley and Bill Barilko of the Toronto Maple Leafs came to the train station to see Whitey (Rimstad)," said Don McLean. "They knew Whitey from the war. It was shortly after that Barilko was killed in a plane crash on a hunting trip in Ontario." Don kept the autographed Empress of France schedule that the two hockey immortals had signed on the back.

England, the best food in Sweden and Switzerland. He called the Swedish and Italians the most hospitable of all the people and the least enjoyable country being Germany, mainly due to snow or rain for every game the Leafs played on the outdoor rinks there. Streatham, England had the largest ice surface, 110x210 and Brussels had the smallest, 47x160. Paris and Milan were the most enjoyable cities according to Obodiac and the best team the Leafs played was a British All-Star squad.

In winning the Churchill Cup in England, the Leafs became the last Canadian team to accomplish this feat. The following year, the Edmonton Mercurys, with Billy Gibson in the lineup and on their way to the Olympic Games gold medal, lost in the Churchill Cup tournament. The Cup was discontinued after that series.

Before they sailed for home, and after winning the Winston Churchill Cup, the Leafs played a series of exhibition games, while some members visited friends. Most played without too much zip, their main goals already behind them.

Bill Flick broke his wrist March 31, as the Leafs played in Wembley, winning 8-4. Of those six exhibition games it was the only one the team won, losing three and tying two. The Leafs suffered three other less-serious injuries during the entire trip, causing Tom Wood, Hec Negrello and Don Vogan to miss a few games.

The Leafs also took in some of the London sites and sounds after the Churchill Cup, including seeing Judy Garland open her English tour. When the Leafs left for home, not everyone got on the returning boat. Shorty Malacko chose to stay behind for a month or two, suiting up for the Harringay Racers of the English Hockey League.

The Leafs had departed on their trip Dec. 17 and returned to Lethbridge via plane on April 19 to a tumultuous welcome by family, friends and fans. But on the way home the Maple Leafs had stopped in Toronto.

Lethbridge's Maple Leafs proved to be a popular team with the fans during their European tour. The players were only getting about five pounds a week to play, as spending money along with their meals, travel and accommodations - all this bounty from tour organizer Bunny Ahearne.

"Five pounds, well . . . we used to spill more than that," Gibby said with a laugh. "There were times over there I'd get Karl (Sorokoski) so drunk I couldn't see him."

But Gibby is quick to add the Leafs didn't have all that much time to party during their four-month, 14-country tour abroad. If they weren't at a game they were checking in and out of hotels and climbing off and on buses, trains and planes. "After the championship game in Paris we drank some champagne, from a place right across the street from the hotel, and then got up the next day and went to the bike races," said Don, one of Gibson's line mates.

Besides Christmas and New Years, the Leafs had a few other days that required a celebration. Hector Negrello, the team's captain, and Karl Sorokoski had birthdays during the trip. McLean remembered when a game in Italy was stopped part way through so they could announce Leafs' Bill Chandler had just become the proud father of a new bambino back in Lethbridge.

"They gave us a gallon of wine and fruit bread so we could celebrate after the game," said Gibby. Upon arrival back in Lethbridge, Tom Wood found out he too was a brand new father.

"Looking back on this once-in-a-lifetime experience, what is most incredible is how It was accomplished and the players who achieved it," writes Tom Wood on the Maple Leaf web-site. "Today Canada sends an NHL All-Star team of millionaire hockey players and Hockey Canada buys them rings if they win.

"By comparison we survived without a sponsor, purchased our own championship rings, and raised pin money by playing extra games in small towns across Europe. Each player received $10 per game, most of which went to the purchase of gifts for our families. Still, I wouldn't trade our experience for all of the money in the world.

"There is no doubt that today's hockey, worldwide, is played at a much higher skill level than it was back then. In addition, there is no question that our team was not as talented as the

NHL teams of that era. But the challenge for us to win was much greater than if they had sent a team from the NHL.

"I would like to pay tribute to our wonderful teammates who were not here (Enamx Centre in 2011) to celebrate the 60th Anniversary of our great victory in Paris on March 17, 1951."

The fact Tom brought forward is the obvious of all - the passing of the players, a change no one wanted to see, yet an inevitable change.

Dick Gray was gone by the time the 50th anniversary rolled around, but he was remembered. Dick was with the Leafs in 1939 and 1940, prior to the war, and then in 1947. He also toiled for the Regina Abbott Generals as a junior and was playing-coach in 1946 with Vancouver Canucks. He signed a pro contract with the Detroit Red Wings, but he wound up in the military service, far away from Canadian hockey rinks, in India.

"I think, if you really want the truth, my most memorable moment of the whole thing was when we beat Melville Millionaires to win the trip to Europe," Dick said, a few years before his death. "Hector scored with 20 seconds to go to make it 3-2, and give us the series in the eighth game. We played all eight games at the old arena, in the spring of 1949. After seven games each club had won two and three games had ended in ties.

"We had arrived home Monday at 7 p.m. from a tournament in Kelowna, and stepped on the ice at 8 p.m. to start that series with Melville. It was ironic the way things turned out. The only job I didn't hold on the club was captain - and I had put up $2,500 for the first three games. Hardly anyone came out to see us play. I turned things over to the Lethbridge Brewery, and the next five games were sold out. When I look back in my scrapbook and see the write-ups from those games it's really

Tom Wood

something. It was my decision that we go to an eighth game, rather than sudden-death after the seventh. It was after that we were asked to represent Canada in Paris at the world championships. Winning the gold medal was nice, but it was nothing compared to winning the trip itself.

"I'm sure the boys would agree another memorable moment was when we won the Winston Churchill trophy in England. We had to score four goals in the third period to win 4-3. The English team we beat was made up of Canadians, but they represented England."

Dick was always an "up-front" person in Lethbridge, involved with the Lethbridge and District Exhibition for many years and active in the cattle industry, though most remembered him for his hockey days, when he was stacking up memories with the Maple Leafs.

Walter "Whitey" Rimstad was once one of this area's finest athletes. In his day Whitey played with, or against, some of hockey's biggest names, men like Garth Busch, Kenny Stewart, Peter Slobodian, Max Bentley, Eddy Wares, Alex Kaleta, Alf Pike and Dutch Hiller.

Whitey singled out Andy Young as "one of the finest athletes" he ever played with, and didn't hesitate to pick the best linemates he centred.

"My best line had to be Don Culley and Mel Lunde," Whitey said some years before his death "I really enjoyed playing with them. During the war I centred Kalita and Culley, and I also enjoyed that line as well."

Whitey's list of accomplishments in hockey was impressive. He and his Lethbridge Maple Leaf teammates earned their way into the Lethbridge, the Alberta and the Hockey Halls of Fame as a result of their world amateur hockey championship.

Herald Photo
Dick Gray at his feedlot in 1979

Though mainly a centre during his hockey career, Whitey patrolled the blue line for the Maple Leafs when the club first went overseas - but soon switched back to his familiar forward spot. He could always put the puck in the net, but at the same time he knew hockey was more than offence and was credited with being a better-than-average defensive player. There is little doubt the world championship with the Maple Leafs was a highlight for Whitey, but he also enjoyed other great moments on ice.

"In 1951, I was the oldest player on the Maple Leafs, and it was still a tremendous thrill to win the world championship. Playing for one's country was a good feeling - it's hard to describe the feeling when they played O Canada the night we won the championship. That was one of the finest moments I've ever had.

"I've really had quite a few thrills in hockey. The first time I played in Madison Square Gardens, in 1936, with the New York Rovers - the Rangers farm club, was really great. Times were pretty tough back then, and coming to New York from Edmonton as a naive boy was really something.

"I guess my first thrill in hockey was my first year in junior when our Edmonton Athletic Club team made it to the Memorial Cup finals, but lost out in overtime in the second game to Toronto St. Mike's. I was 17 then."

Whitey finished his junior career in Edmonton and played four years with the Rovers before moving to the Lethbridge Maple Leafs. Then came World War II, and some hockey memories, playing with the likes of Bentley, Stewart, Lude and cohorts. Stationed in Calgary, he played in a league that included Lethbridge, an air force team, and a navy squad as well as his army club.

Whitey played with the Lethbridge Maple Leafs in 1940-42, in the old Western Senior

League, which included Trail and Calgary, before he joined the army. "We won the Alberta championship my first year with the Leafs, but were beat out by Regina – they eventually went on to win the Allan Cup," he said. "The second year we won Alberta again, but lost to Port Arthur, again the eventual Allan Cup champions.

His year with the Maple Leafs' world championship club was his last as a hockey player, except for the odd old-timers game.

"In the army I played with some fine clubs, that's for sure," he said. "Those teams were full of professionals and top amateurs. But as far as team spirit, nothing could compare to the Maple Leafs. When we won the world championship the spirit of the club was really something. We had real harmony, it's hard to describe. I really enjoyed my experiences in hockey, and all the people I met and played hockey with."

The snow-white crop of hair, the wide grin, and the bubbling personality of Whitey Rimstad were evident in Lethbridge sports circles for many years. He supported local sports such as hockey, baseball or horse racing, watching others build memorable moments, much the way a past generation watched Whitey racking his memories.

Billy Gibson, who died in the summer of 2006, went to his grave with something no other person in Lethbridge has ever earned - an Olympic Gold Medal. He earned that medal in 1952, skating for the Edmonton Mercurys at the Olympic hockey championships. While the medal meant a lot to Gibby, it didn't serve as his most memorable moment in hockey.

"In any athlete's life the

Herald Photo
Walter "Whitey" Rimstad

Herald Photo
Billy Gibson shows off his Olympic Gold

Olympic gold medal is the pinnacle," Gibby pointed out. "In Europe the medal places the athlete close to royalty.

"It is terribly important over there - and it is important to me as well. But, I'd have to say my greatest experience was my first trip to Europe with the Lethbridge Maple Leafs, when we won the world hockey championship.

"That was the highlight of my life. It wasn't that we won as much as it was the way we had to work for everything.

"At home, we'd practice on Sundays, after the public skating, and we'd clean the ice before and after. We bought our own equipment, sticks, etc., and even paid to have our skates sharpened. When we heard that if we won the Western Canadian title we could go on to the world championships things started to become a reality. Without the efforts of men like Tom Kirkham of the Lethbridge Jaycees, Harold Brandeth, president of the Alberta Amateur Hockey Association, or zone representative J. T. North of High River, we wouldn't have gone.

"The reason the trip was so important to me was I knew how hard we all worked to get it. On the other hand the Mercurys were sponsored all the way in 1952. We raised everything as Leafs, and including Jaycee donations we earned up to $10,000. That put us on the way. Once there we played exhibition games to raise spending money.

"We were gone four months up to the time we won the world championship in Paris. One game we had to put on our uniforms in a hospital. The rink was a huge open sheet of ice with boards on one side and a plank for boards on the other. We played in rain. We played in snow. Once we played in snow so bad we'd play for five minutes, scrape the ice for 10, and then play again. And we had 16,000 people watching us that day.

"I had many things to be thankful for in sports, from my years coming up, to the years with the Native Sons and then into the Lethbridge Maple Leaf organization.

"A fastball thrill was when I played with Shaughnessy Cadillacs in 1953 or 1954 and we lost the Western Canadian championship in Vancouver to the Girodays.

"My greatest disappointment had to come when we were supposed to fly to Moscow with the Leafs. We were in Sweden in the morning, and were supposed to have played in Moscow in the afternoon, and then fly back to Sweden. But politics reared its head and we didn't go. I would have loved to play against the Russians.

"I don't believe too many people realize what it means to represent your country at a world championship. The people and the government, should be made aware of the importance, and of the pressure on the individual. Athletics is a gift and it brings pressures.

"Yes, I've had lots of great moments in sports, but when it comes right down to it it's the people involved that really count, the ones you play with, and against." Billy Gibson always had a quip and a story, always seemed to be happy, and cherished his days with the Lethbridge Maple Leafs and the Edmonton Mercurys.

Roger Kahn wrote about his *Boys of Summer,* the great ol' Brooklyn Dodger team. To me the Lethbridge Maple Leafs of 1951 were the Boys of Winter.

The Leafs were an experience everyone shared in, the players, the city and a 10-year-old north side kid who is proud to say he grew up to know most of the Maple Leafs. The Leafs' legacy will live on, and hopefully this collection of thoughts will help sustain the legend.

The Native Sons

Way back when I was a kid – my kids think they hadn't even invented the puck in those days – hockey equipment was relatively simple, especially if you played shinny on the streets, or even games at the Adams outdoor rink.

After you had the skates, usually second hand, you were on your way. Sticks could be picked up from Native Son stars, like Andy Drobut, Guyle Fielder, Aut Erickson, Gus Adams or Billy Voss after games or as they walked to the arena. I even got a prize goalie stick from Sons netminder Seth Martin. They may have been cracked, but they were still useable for shinny, with the help of a nail or two and some tape in the right place - maybe even a few support slats down each side. And they'd last.

Those are probably my first memories of the Native Sons, because most of the above mentioned walked past my house on the way to games - with suits, ties and long overcoats.

The Native Sons were Lethbridge's answer to the Maple Leafs of senior hockey fame. The Sons games were where everyone went on a Saturday night. The old Arena was jammed as fans gathered to cheer on the beloved Sons, always hoping they'd make it to the Memorial Cup Finals - and perhaps win!

Like all great teams, the sum of their success is in their players, and these are just some of the best of the best.

Today, hockey sticks cost what my parents used to pay for my skates. And speaking of skates, how many kids did you know who wore some girl's, likely a sister's, castoff figure skates, dyed black? Not me fortunately; I was an only child.

Then there were the pads. There was no such thing as a jock strap and protective equipment that went with it. You just jammed some socks in your shorts. Shin pads were made from Eaton's catalogues or cardboard or magazines, held in place by rubber sealer rings.

I was lucky in that Brian Wardman gave me his old football shoulder pads and I could use them for hockey. I was one of the few with upper-body protection. But, when you were as skinny as I was at age 10 you needed all the protection you could get.

Gloves could be anything from canvas summer garden gloves, swiped from your mother and filled with balled-up paper, wool mitts, or if you were really lucky as I was, some holey, beat up, but still useable, real live hockey gloves. They were passed on from another parent whose son had grown out of them. In those days people didn't throw anything away, or hold yard sales. Things were passed on and on and on.

It was about my early teens that hockey started to become organized and the minor hockey system came into being. That meant a need for real equipment. My buddy Fred Leslie and I used to sit the bench for the Lethbridge minor league Canadiens for the one year I played. It wasn't that we didn't have good equipment, we just couldn't crack the lineup - on my part, because I couldn't skate. But, bench rider or not, that Christmas I received fibreglass shin pads and even hockey pants. I only played one year. It didn't take me long to know I wasn't the new Rocket Richard or Guyle Fielder.

The Native Sons were special in my eyes, and none more so than Earl Ingarfield. Then Earl went on to play for my favourite NHL team, the New York Rangers, and that made him even more special. Even to this day, I'm still in awe when I talk to Earl or am in his presence.

Billy Voss was another favourite Native Son - he used to room with my Uncle Alec Allison. Then there were the likes of Andy Drobut and Gus Adams, who played street hockey with us for a minute or two in their long overcoats, as they walked to the Arena past our house for games and practices. In those days junior hockey players were among the best-dressed guys in town.

To this day I still admire Steve Arisman, as smooth a player as they came, and still a true gentleman. I remember Les Colwill when Les was playing with the Rangers and he sent Don Pilling a letter, saying that Don had more ice in his drink than Les was seeing with the Rangers. And do you remember Tommy Wood or Rock Crawford - the player who used to stand up on his toes behind the net and "run" to the blueline?

I had a closer look at one of the Sons as a kid -

you could almost say we were pals, well, really acquaintances. You see, Autry Erickson's parents, Bud and Joyce Erickson, lived on 12th Street C North, right on my paper route, and off and on I'd see Aut as I delivered The Herald to the house. But deeper than that, Bud was a member of the Oddfellows Lodge, as was the entire Allison family, so Aut and I intermingled at the annual Christmas party and other Oddfellow family gatherings. In fact I recall Aut and his sister singing at the Christmas functions for a number of years - until Aut outgrew those types of public appearances and picked up a hockey stick instead.

Aut played for a year with the Lethbridge Native Sons in the late 1950s, along with Earl Ingarfield I believe, before he went to play in Prince Albert, with the Mintos for the next two seasons. Autry moved up to the NHL in 1960 with the Boston Bruins, where he played the next two seasons – remember this was the time when there were only six teams in the NHL and you had to be a great player to make it into the league, like other Lethbridgeites: Ingarfield, Stasiuk, Colwill, and Doug Barkley. Doug had a promising NHL career cut short by an eye injury.

When Autry went to the NHL it was the era when stay-at-home defencemen was the code. He also suited up for three games with the Chicago Blackhawks in 1962-1963 and played another 34 games with the Blackhawks in 1963-1964. A highlight in his career included playing with the Toronto Maple Leafs for the 1967 Stanley Cup. After his playing days were over, he coached the Phoenix Roadrunners. Autry finished his hockey career as the Assistant General Manager for the New York Islanders.

Aut played in an era when the penalty shot was first introduced, and the opposing coach could select any player off the other team to take the shot. While playing with Boston, Autry, a low-scoring defenceman, was selected to take the shot - and he scored!

Autry possessed a bruising defensive game. He played in 226 NHL games with the Boston Bruins, Chicago Blackhawks, Toronto Maple Leafs and the Oakland Seals, scoring seven goals and 31 points to go along with 182 penalty minutes. Autry left his mark in the NHL through his unrelenting defensive play. Anyone who crossed the blueline on his side paid the price of his vice-like grip or a resounding bounce off the boards, taking them out of the play. The blonde-haired, six-foot, 180-pound blueliner always brought a gritty game to the ice, be it on our 16th Street rink, in junior hockey or in the NHL.

"He wasn't an offensive player and he didn't have a big, booming shot. But he was great defensively," said Vic Stasiuk, another Lethbridge northsider who made it to the NHL. "We played baseball on the north side and we were neighbours in Boston for a year (1960-1961). Aut was big and strong and was like a vice grip once he got to you."

Earl Ingarfield a former Native Son teammate with Autry said: "He and I were very good friends and we always stayed in touch. When he went to the Boston Bruins and I was with the (New York) Rangers, if there was a chance, we would get together and have dinner."

"He was a competitor and he was tough," said Ingarfield. "He was a solid player, nothing fancy. But boy, did he do his job. Once out on the ice though the friendship ended."

In his most productive offensive season Aut scored four goals and 15 points in 65 games with the Seals in 1967-1968 before wrapping up his playing days in Oakland in 1970.

After his playing career Autry coached the Phoenix Roadrunners from 1970 to 1972 and finished his hockey career as the assistant general manager for the New York Islanders.

Once leaving hockey Erickson was involved in real estate around Scottsdale, Arizona, and in California. "We were always in touch," said Earl. "We'd vacation down in Rancho Mirage and Aut and his family were just outside Palm Springs. We'd see him every year down there and did for many years."

Autry passed away August 21, 2010, at his home in Moreno Valley, California, at age 72 after a long battle with cancer.

I have always stood in awe of Earl Ingarfield. Earl was the star of the Native Sons when I was a kid and I never got over that idol thing.

Earl was one of the finest skating Native Son, whirling and stick-handling through opposition lineups, not being hit - and scarcely needing to hit himself.

One of my great moments these past few years came when I was asked to write a letter of recommendation for Earl's induction into the Alberta Spots Hall of Fame in 2007. I'm pleased to say he was accepted. An even prouder moment came a few weeks later when Earl sent me a signed picture as thanks for the small part I played.

They say fact should never interfere with legends, and a great Earl Ingarfield story dates to his days with the Sons. It seems the Sons trailed by two goals, and Earl's father, Harry Ingarfield, told his son if he tied up the game and scored the winner he'd give him a race horse. Earl fulfilled his father's wishes. Now, you might wonder as to the truth of this - but one stick to build your house with is the fact Harry Ingarfield was known to frequent the race track.

You have to ask yourself, legend or fact? Me, I'll stick with the legend, thinking it's a fact.

One of the few times I covered a Lethbridge Broncos game, was when Earl was first coaching - hockey was always Pat Sullivan's beat - the Broncos lost, and the refereeing was pathetic, to be kind. As Earl came down the chute from the players' bench I was waiting, and I asked him about the refs. He was still mad, and he said enough to fill my column for a week.

I wrote it all up, and the next day Earl was even madder. The league had read his rantings and fined him $1,500. I think he was pleased when Sully was back on the Bronco beat.

New York City - the "Big Apple." What better place to begin a career? That's where Earl, the former Native Son star player, began what turned out to be a 13-year National Hockey League career. "Inky" played with the New York Rangers for nine seasons, at one time teaming with Dean Prentice and Andy Bathgate to form one of the most potent lines in hockey's long history.

He also served a year and a half with the Pittsburgh Penguins and another two and half seasons with the Oakland Seals. During his NHL tenure "Inky" fired home 174 goals and picked up 218 assists.

Earl witnessed a lot of exciting events, and has been part of many of them during his hockey life. "I really enjoyed playing, right through to my final two seasons in California. We met some fine people along the way, and that really adds to things. We made a lot of friends, and we still have them."

When Inky's active days were over he turned to coaching and handled the Regina Pats of the Western Canada Hockey League for some time before moving into the head-coaching role with the New York Islanders for two years. He returned

Photograph autographed to me
by Earl "Inky" Ingarfield

home to Lethbridge and coached the Lethbridge Broncos of the WCHL for two seasons before leaving hockey to turn his attentions to business interests, as well as a long tenure as a scout and adviser for the New York Islanders. Among his New York Islander recruits was the great Bryan Trottier.

In later years Earl's son, Earl Jr. was a star with the Lethbridge Broncos and went on to briefly play for the Calgary Flames in the NHL. "I'm not bothered by comparisons with my father," Earl Jr. told me during the Flames try-out camp. "I have so much respect for my father."

In 2007, Earl Sr. was named to the Alberta Sports Hall of Fame, an honour long overdue. Like Earl, another Lethbridge NHL great, Vic Stasiuk, had to wait until well into the early 2000s to be inducted into the Alberta Spots Hall of Fame.

Vic played with the Boston Bruins for six years in the NHL and also enjoyed successful stints with the Detroit Red Wings, and the team he broke in with, Chicago Black Hawks.

But his sparkling years came with the Uke line in Boston, his 16 goals in Stanley Cup playoff competition, and being with the Detroit Red Wings in three Stanley Cup championships. These stick out as the most memorable moments in Vic's long hockey career.

Vic noted, "I never really thought about it before, but I guess the most exciting personal feeling I experienced, the one that means the most, would be the moment the coach of the Kansas City Playmores said 'pack your trunks, you're going to Chicago Black Hawks to stay.'

"It wasn't a fun occasion, but that moment was quite a personal experience for me," Vic recalled. "The next great feeling came standing on the blue line for my first game against the Boston Bruins, anticipating what it was going to be like to play my first game in the National Hockey League.

"That call in my room, with Bob Goodacre from Red Deer and Eddy Lear from Winnipeg sitting there, back in January of the 1949-50 season, was the highlight of my life at that time. I've had a lot of highlights since, but I think that one is still the most memorable one.

"I think the Cup victories were more of a team experience than an individual one, and even the Cup goals were not that much more exciting than the other ones."

Vic began his career in Lethbridge with Ed Bruchet's Native Sons, and during his 14 years in the NHL scored 186 regular season goals. He had always dreamed of playing in the NHL and when his playing days ended he came back to coach in the league, handling Philadelphia Flyers and the Vancouver Canucks. He spent six years coaching in the minor leagues before moving back to the NHL with the Flyers. Upon leaving the Canucks Vic left hockey for a while but returned to coach

Earl Ingarfield and Bernie "Boom Boom" Geoffrion

"The most memorable moment for me was the first time I skated onto the ice at Madison Square Garden for the first New York Ranger home game in 1958," Earl remembered. *"Hearing those 17,500 fans raising the roof, before the game even started, when the Rangers skated onto the ice, was thrilling. I didn't play very much in that first game, but I was just happy to make the team.*

"Everybody stood up and cheered us, what enthusiasm! The excitement stayed throughout my career. I really enjoyed it, right through to my final two seasons in California."

the Taber Golden Suns in the Alberta junior league and then the Medicine Hat Tigers in the Western Canada Hockey League.

Vic enjoyed many memorable moments in hockey through the years, but one of his most memorable experiences came when he attained his dream - to play in the NHL.

As the 1930s were closing, coal mining expanded as the No. 8 mine atop the west side coulee in Lethbridge began operation. For Vic Stasiuk the memories of No. 8 mine still centre on his little red wagon. He was forever pulling that wagon up and down the coulee hills, heading from his north side home to No. 8 mine and back again. He laughs as he says he has more than 200 of those trips under his belt.

"I'd pull that little wagon down the coulees, across the old car bridge, along the road to the slag dump for No. 8, and back again. The old highway bridge was just north of the present Highway 3 crossing. You could go, as the crow flies, up the coulees to the old CPR roundhouse, going straight east along the coulee. I had to pull that wagon up and down those coulees, full of coal, but even that little bit of coal would help out."

Vic would sometimes just follow his dad and they'd pick through the slack together. One day Vic decided he should climb much higher up the side of the smoldering dump. "It was real loose, and as you climbed you'd slip and slip," says Vic. "Some of the loose stuff would roll all the way down to the bottom. Luckily my dad was with me this day, because as I climbed and dug into the loose coal to find some lumps, all of a sudden I disappeared. I sank in right up to my hips, and it was starting to get hot too. I had slipped through the slack into a kind of seam - this pile was always smoldering and steaming. My dad scrambled up and pulled me out of there. If he hadn't my legs literally would have been toast."

One of the family's moves was to 16th Street North, right across from the old outdoor hockey rink. That, he says, is why he became a hockey player, having easy and quick access to the ice. He laughs as he tells of ditching his violin in the back porch, grabbing his skates, and heading for the rink instead of music lessons.

Vic says the family would often get together around the stove and enjoy cabbage rolls Mother Stasiuk made on a regular basis, as well as borscht, always in a heated pot on the back burner. "Every place we lived had a coal cook stove, with a cabinet up top and four burner areas, and on the side it had a water tank where you'd get warm water. There was a single pipe with a tap when you wanted your bath filled - a big old galvanized tub, which you later shared the water with the other brothers and sisters. Things were tough in those days.

"Between 16th and 17th Street my dad also ran 50 to 60 milk cows. I'd take them down to the coulees, water them, let them graze and pick up a little coal too. We'd also sneak a couple of squirts of milk in a can for our own use before we'd herd them back. They always knew their way back up the coulees to home, because they knew they were going to be milked."

Through the years Vic and I have crossed paths many times. Best of all though were when he had his farm in the river valley and raised the finest sweet corn you ever tasted. He passed along more than a few dozen of those sweet cobs to me, and I enjoyed every one of them.

Another great day came in 2008 when the sports media gathered at Paradise Canyon - once Vic's farm - for the announcement he had been inducted into the Alberta Sports Hall of Fame. As with Earl Ingarfield, the honour was long ovedue.

Vic marvels at the fact he was fortunate to play with the likes of Alex Delveccio and Gordie Howe during those great years in Detroit. But on the other end, he wasn't too excited about his coaching days in Philadelphia, where the players paid little attention to a coach who was earning a third their salary.

Vic is amazed how many calls he still gets

from reporters in the former cities he played in seeking a look into the past. He still regularly receives letters from fans seeking autographed pictures.

I've always enjoyed Vic's summation of the old World Hockey Association. He once looked up at a flock of seagulls when he was on his tractor, and said, "that's what that league was like, flying in every direction and never hitting anyone."

Vic came before my sharp memory time with the Native Sons. But during Earl's and Autry's days with the Sons there were others who caught my attention, like Freddie Sasakamoose from the Moose Jaw Canucks and Len Lunde of the Edmonton team.

Other Sons, like Seth Martin, the great goalie who did play a while in St. Louis with the Blues, and their fiery coach Ed Bruchet, are memorable.

Then, of course, there was Glidin' Guyle Fielder and Doug Barkley. An eye injury cut Barkley's NHL career with Detroit off in an instant. Most say he was one of the best and would be an All-Star for years to come. Visors were few and far between unfortunately in his day.

I met Sasakamoose a couple of times at the

annual Kaiani Golf Tournament in Waterton. We talked of his time in the NHL with Chicago Blackhawks and how he suddenly left the team to return to his home. He was homesick.

I mentioned Freddie Sasakamoose to Vic Stasiuk and he remembered him from his 'Hawks days as a potent goal scorer.

Freddie was always a threat when on the ice when playing against the Native Sons. He was a memorable player. How else would a young boy remember a rival team star? As well, Freddie was a great golfer and was always one of the men to beat at the Kainai Invitational – not that I was ever in that position.

The Kainai Invitational was quite an event, featuring among the top shot-makers Willie Littlechild of Hobbema, a winner of the Tom Longboat Trophy as the top Indian athlete in Canada, and later on a Member of Parliament.

A nice aspect of the tournament was the barbecue, where everyone sat around and told stories, some true, others stretched a fair bit, especially from Willie.

As just a kid, I got to know Guyle Fielder on a personal basis when he was still playing for the Native Sons, mainly because at one time he was courting my uncle Al Walton's daughter Bev. Al was the pro at the Henderson Lake Golf Course at the time, and Fielder would come out to the course to play golf, and see Bev.

I recall Al saying once, "you can always tell when Fielder has been here, half my beer is gone."

To this day I still admire Steve Arisman, as smooth a player as they came with the Native Sons, and still a true gentleman.

Steve's smooth, free-wheeling, take charge style saw him score a bus load of goals and win over many fans during his days with the Sons.

He probably gained the most fans during the playoffs in 1952 when he experienced his most memorable moment as a Native Son. "I would have to say that came when we were playing against the Edmonton Oil Kings," said Steve.

"In the second game of that series we had St. Boniface 6-4, but then we picked up a penalty. At that time you had to serve the full two minutes even if the other team scored. They scored four times in 72 seconds and beat us 8-6."

Steve toiled four years with the Sons, patrolling the right wing and scoring 106 goals. He had the opportunity to turn professional with the

New York Rangers, but chose not to go.

A former Recreation Co-ordinator for the City of Lethbridge, Steve stayed deeply involved in community activities. One of the last times I saw Steve was when he and I were involved as a torch bearers for the Alberta Senior Games in Lethbridge in 2008.

One thing about Steve, from the first day I met him through to today, he is a true gentleman.

Many decades after he skated with the New York Rangers of the National Hockey League, former Native Son Les Colwill had many cherished memories.

Les began his hockey career with Lethbridge Knights of Columbus midgets, coached by Syd Hall, and then spent four years with the Lethbridge Native Sons before signing a professional contract with the Rangers and heading for the Saskatoon Quakers.

"Probably my biggest thrill came when Earl Ingarfield and I were picked up by the Regina Pats for the the Memorial Cup," said Colwill. "Regina beat us out, then they picked Earl and I up and we went on to beat St. Boniface. Murray Armstrong

"We had managed to make the playoffs that year, and the Oil Kings were one of the favoured clubs to win the Memorial Cup. They had won the league and we had finished fourth. In the deciding game in Edmonton it was 3-3 late in the third period. We came out of our own end with a rink-length rush and I believe it was Billy Dea who gave me the puck. I scored what turned out to be the winning goal and that goal gave us the series. That was a dandy series that year. We went on to beat out Flin Flon, but we lost in seven games to St. Boniface in the Western finals, for the Abbott Cup."

Steve Arisman

was the Pats' coach back then. We lost out in the finals in seven games to Toronto Marlboros for the Memorial Cup. I scored a goal and had a few assists.

"Those thrills were in sport, but my biggest thrill in life had to be at Williamsport, Louisiana when I watched a Lethbridge team in the Little League World Series. It was a big thrill to watch those kids march onto the field - there were 30,000 people but those kids only knew the six of us fathers. There was more feeling in that moment than anything else."

Les spent one year with the Rangers, scoring seven goals and picking up six assists, back in the 1958-59 season when the NHL was a six-team loop. I remember when he sent Herald Sports Editor Don Pilling a letter, telling Don he had more ice in his drink than he was seeing with the Rangers. After his professional hockey career Les Colwill became a three-decade employee with Sicks Lethbridge Brewery.

And who can forget Native Sons like Tommy Wood - later a Maple Leaf - smoothie Billy Dea and Rock Crawford. He used to stand up on his toes and behind the net and "run" to the blueline. Other players sure got out of his way.

The stories of the Native Sons, their rise as a team to the Abbott Cup Finals, one step from the Memorial Cup Finals, where they lost out to St. Boniface, are great ones.

I recall standing on the old 9th Street Bridge to watch the Sons train come in from St. Bobiface, and then rushing down to take pictures of the stars, with my mother's camera. Well, I had the camera wrong way round, and instead of the star players, I had 14 photos of my distorted nose staring down into the camera.

What is best about the Native Sons era, at least to me, is I became friends with four of their greatest, Earl, Vic, Autry and Steve.

41

Remembering the old Lethbridge Arena

"Ninety years ago, in January 1923, the Lethbridge Ice Arena opened at 2nd Ave. and 12th A Street South.," says Lethbridge Historical Society Past-President Belinda Crowson.

"There were literally hundreds of events held in the old wood frame Lethbridge Arena. But the most memorable, certainly for those who were there, would likely be the night it burned to the ground. In just over 90 minutes, March 12, 1971, the 49-year-old arena was destroyed by flames as 1,800 hockey fans streamed from the blazing building.

"Early in the third period, at the 19-second mark, with the hometown Sugar Kings trailing the Edmonton Maple Leafs 2-1, fire was spotted beneath the wooden seats in the southeast corner of the building, the only section with hardly any fans. Within minutes flames engulfed the building and the roof caved in on dozens of framed hockey and sports photographs in the lobby - though many were saved by quick-thinking fans - leaving only memories of 49 years of use.

"During the blaze the night of March 12, Capt. William Short of the fire department received burns to one hand and his face. Fire fighters had to soak their clothes to keep them from catching fire in the intense heat and most of the windows along the north side of the Elk's Club, to the south across the alley from the arena, were shattered by the heat."

I have always believed Sugar Kings' public address announcer, Hans DeGroot, was directly responsible for the fact no one panicked when the fire was spotted. He quietly asked patrons to exit the building by the west and north exits, never once mentioning the word "fire" during his calm directives.

Sugar King manager Syd Hall made arrangements for the playoff series to continue in Taber, a town which ironically had also lost its arena a few years earlier, as had Medicine Hat. To facilitate fans, Northern Bus Lines ran buses to Taber from the city, for $2 a person. The proceeds were to go to the Sugar Kings to help offset their property losses in the fire.

Among the Sugar King players playing that night were future NHL stars Lanny McDonald, who remembers the incident right to the time, and John

Davidson. Other teammates included Len Chalmers, George McCrea, Randy Andreachuck, Dave George and Ken Dodd. The Sugar Kings went on to beat Edmonton the next two games in Taber, by identical 4-2 scores.

It would be four years before the old wooden structure would be replaced in the city, with the opening of the Canada Winter Games Sportsplex in 1975.

The building had been home ice to the 1951 world champion Lethbridge Maple Leafs, the Lethbridge Native Sons and the Sugar Kings, and teams like the New York Rangers had graced its ice surface. Lethbridge hockey legends like Guyle Fielder, Earl Ingarfield, Vic Stasiuk, Pete Slobodian, Bob Kirkpatrick, Eddie Dorohoy and Bill Ramsden all skated on arena ice.

"The arena had housed the Shirtsleeve Curling Bonspiel before the Civic Ice Centre opened, and the artificial ice in the arena marked the first time in Canada

man-made ice had been used for curling," says Belinda.

Spike Martell was long associated with the building as its ice maker and supervisor. He was also the head man of the rink rats, a crew of young boys who cleaned the ice between periods of the hockey games. Doug Harrold, Richie Cuell, Jerry Malakow and Pat Sullivan were among the rink rat crew.

The arena was built in 1922, for $23,000 and had natural ice. In 1937 Milk River businessman Herman Thole bought the building from the city, for $18,000, enlarged it and installed artificial ice.

Seating capacity of the building was increased

Photo Courtesy of Galt Archives

from 1,800 to 3,000 and improvements were made to lower the ice surface to improve slope and provide a better view for spectators. New dressing rooms were constructed, as well as office space, coffee counter and main entrance. The length of the ice was expanded to make it 185 feet by 80 feet in size.

By 1963 the city bought the structure back, for $47,000. In 1965 it underwent a major refurbishing, for $171,000. The arena was officially reopened by Mayor Frank Sherring. More upgrading had been planned for 1975.

Besides hockey, the arena played host to the Ice Follies, Boy Scout Ice Rodeos, penny carnivals and wrestlers, the likes of Primo Carnera, Whipper Billy Watson, Hard Boiled Haggerty and Pete Shologan the Coaldale Cossack.

One of the war-year's greatest entertainers, Gracie Fields, graced the arena stage, singing her hits including Christopher Robin and the Biggest Aspidistra in the World. Slim Whitman, Webb Pierce, Porter Wagoner, Jim Reeves, Brenda Lee and Gene Autry and his horse Champion all stood on the arena's make- shift stage as did CBC radio's Happy Gang. Gene Krupa, Jimmy Dorsey and Spike Jones wooed fans in the grand old building and many a dollar was raised during Victory Bond Drives. Horse shows, band festivals, world champion figure skater Don Jackson, political boss William Aberhart, the Coldstream Guards and baseball great Bob Feller were all part of the arena's history.

The Kinsmen Sportsmen's Dinners

There have been many acclaimed athletic visitors to our city, on their own, as teams and certainly through the Kinsmen Sportsmen's Dinners and later for some, the LDS Father and Son Banquets. All proved fuel for the many sports stories told around the tables in coffee shops and bars for years to come.

For me, as a young person working at The Lethbridge Herald with aspirations to be the Sports Editor, there was nothing grander than the Kinsmen Sportsmen's Dinners. Being a sports fan I was in heaven when the super-stars of sports came to town. It was because of Don Pilling and his talks with Jack McRea at the Ad-Viser, I managed to have an inside track to many of the dinners. Eventually I was there writing only for the Ad-Viser, mainly interviewing the boxers and cowboys. I even got in quite a few years ahead of the age minimum of 21 years.

In 1959, Lefty Gomez, the Hall of Fame pitcher for the Yankees was a guest. I didn't meet him then, but some years later he was at a baseball tournament in Whitefish, Montana. We sat together for some of the games and talked about baseball of course. I also drove him back and forth to his hotel. It took me a while to realize who I was talking with at first, and from then on it was a baseball fan's dream.

The Kinsmen dinners featured the best. They were a sport fan's dream. I attended a good number – and each year in my mind that number seems to grow. Thanks to Jack McCrea and Don Pilling I was able to worm my way into places I shouldn't have been, and as a result was able to meet many of the stars close-up and personal at the pre-dinner fete in the Sick's Brewery's Snake Room, overseen by Spike Martell.

I was privileged, through Reno Lizzi and Don Pilling, to be in the presence of sport super-stars the likes of Roy Campenella and Sandy Koufax. I traded barbs with the likes of Gene Kiniski and Rocky Marciano and interviewed Jake LaMotta, Carmen Basillio, Archie Moore and Joey Giardello - all men of boxing whom I idolized, all who were in Lethbridge as guests of the Kinsmen Sportsmen's Dinner.

Certainly, as far as the Lethbridge Sports scene is concerned, no moment rivals the winning of the world's hockey championship in 1951 by the Lethbridge Maple Leafs. But there were other big moments, including the prestigious Kinsmen Sportsmen's Dinners, which ran for 20 years; and for basketball fans there was the era of the Broder Chinooks; and hockey also had the thrills provided by the Native Sons.

In 1953 Don Pilling and Hugh Buchanan, the Sports Editor and Managing Editor respectively of The Lethbridge Herald at the time and its publisher by 1954, were discussing the possibility of a sports banquet being held in this city. Pilling mentioned the idea to Bus Murdoch, at the time the city's first athletic director and a member of the Kinsmen Club.

"Bus took the idea to the Kinsmen, they discussed things, and they thought it would be a good idea," Pilling said. "Initially the banquet was held at the Marquis Hotel, where it stayed for the first two years. But the Marquis was small, with room for only 200 to 210 people, so it moved to the Civic Sports Centre, which could hold 500 people.

"As the attendance continued to grow the banquet was moved to the LCC Barn, then called the Whoop-Up Pavilion and owned by Murdoch, which held about 800 to 900 people. Then it went out to the Exhibition Pavilion, and that's where it stayed.

"While Reno Lizzi wasn't involved at the very outset, he was certainly a key person with the dinner for many, many of the following years. What a job he did. I cannot say enough about him."

The first dinner, at $10 a plate, was held at the Marquis, where the guests also stayed in the hotel. It was Jan. 15, 1954, and dinner chairman Jim Crane and his committee brought back former Lethbridge sportscaster Henry Viney as the emcee. The Kinsmen lined up a head table consisting of one of Canada's truly great sports columnists, Jim Coleman; Al Ritchie, Regina sportsman and coach; Normie Kwong and Rollie Miles of the Edmonton Eskimos; Sam Etchevery, quarterback of the Montreal Alouettes; and George Vogan and Harper Parry of the Western Junior Hockey League.

In later years the guests stayed at the El Rancho, where many an after-banquet party was held in rooms throughout the sprawling motel. In its final years, the Park Plaza served as home base for the dinner's functions and guests.

"The dinner went on to become recognized as THE premiere sportsmen's dinner in Canada," said Pilling, relating that Cleveland Indian pitching great Bob Feller, a 1956 guest, said it was one of the best banquets he had been to in his entire life. In later years guests like Rocky Marciano, Gil Hodges and Mel Allan said they were amazed a city this size could support such a show.

Henry Viney emceed the most banquets, 11, including the first one and the final one. The man in charge of the microphone proved to be a key to keeping the banquet flowing.

Ernie Afaganis was the master of ceremonies for five banquets, while Don Pilling, Al McCann, Calgary Stampeder football star Normie Kwong, and sportscaster Doug Smith (the year Viney became a head table guest in 1957) all had the job for one dinner.

Henry Viney

The athletes would come in on a Friday, mainly because Lethbridge was not served by a major airline or on a major highway. They'd be feted by the Kinsmen Friday night, meet the media at a special luncheon in the Sick's Brewery Snake Room Saturday afternoon, do nine or 10 interviews, speak at the dinner Saturday night, and be gone by Sunday.

But, in that short span, they left an indelible mark on the sports fans of southern Alberta, and in particular the Kinsmen and the press, with whom they had the most contact. But Lethbridge also left its mark on them.

One of the key men behind the Kinsmen Sportsmen's Dinners - at least their longevity -

was Reno Lizzi, perhaps the biggest sports fan of them all.

The proceeds of the Kinsmen's dinners went to club projects, but many years there wasn't enough to pass on due to the cost of bringing the guests into town. In reality, the club's major project was the dinner.

The banquet also served as a means of honouring Lethbridge's Sportsmen and Athletes of the year, the winners announced at each banquet.

The Kinsmen movement began in Canada in 1930, when a small group of men in Hamilton, Ontario came together. Today there are clubs from Newfoundland to Vancouver Island. It is an all-Canadian Service Club affiliated throughout the world with the Round Table Clubs of Great Britain, Europe and Africa, with the Apex Clubs of Australia and the Active 20/30 Clubs of the United States.

The Lethbridge Kinsmen Club gained its charter in 1933, and was the 13th Club in Canada. It actively participated in the Second World War by assisting National Kinsmen provide dental clinics and 50 million quarts of milk for the children in Britain. Through the years the Kinsmen have provided funding for national projects such as combating Cystic Fibrosis, polio, mental illness and the construction of a massive housing development in Hong Kong.

Locally, each year the Kinsmen spent $10,000 on the community's greatest need. The Kinsmen is a key organization in the city and have supported numerous clubs and events, including minor football, baseball, hockey, boxing and lacrosse, and backed memberships in the YMCA for underprivileged children. The club has developed ice centres and parks in the city, including Indian Battle Park and in Canada's Centennial Year (1967) helped establish Fort Whoop-Up in the river valley. The dinner helped raise funds for many of these projects.

Dinner guests were selected by their prominence in the sporting community and their immediate successes - such as the World Series MVP. Historical figures were also named to the head table, such as hockey's Cyclone Taylor. Due to its timing in January or February, the dinner was in the middle of the hockey season and few active players were selected.

"In retrospect, I think my timing was good when it came to the dinner," said Reno in my late 1990s interview. "You could make contact with the athletes then. Now it's all through agents. That's why there's no more Kinsmen dinners. Those who still do have sportsmen's dinners can only afford to have one guest, not a dozen like we had.

"I often wonder about how successful it would have been today, but you could never afford to put together head tables like we had. Maybe it will come back some day, but I don't think so."

The problem now is contacting the athletes themselves and then paying the bill. The most Reno and his committees paid was $1,000, but by the final dinner the fee was up to $5,000, resulting in fewer guests. Today, more than 40 years after the last banquet, the fee would likely be 10 times as great.

Gayle Sayers, a National Football League legend and one of the super stars Reno corralled, was a mere $300. His agreement came during the football season, shortly before Sayers set the record for six touchdowns in one game. But nothing changed. He stayed committed to Lethbridge, and the fee.

For decades Reno was certainly one of Lethbridge's best-known sportsmen and haberdashers. Reno began working in the clothing business about 1950, downtown at Nick's Men's Wear, owned by Nick Supina.

"The store was on 3rd Avenue South next to the Club Cigar Store and the Maple Leaf Restaurant," said Reno, perhaps the city's most devoted baseball fan - particularly of the Los Angeles Dodgers. "When I left Supina I went into selling made-to-measure clothes out of my home. Then, in September, 1951, I opened Reno's Haberdashery on 6th Street South, across from the telegraph office and next to Blenner-Hassett's and Mike Hanzel's Shoe Repair on the other side."

In 1959, Reno's closed and Reno joined John Black as a partner. He later teamed up with Paul Ruznack and the pair operated

Black's Men's Wear until Reno retired in 1987.

Through the 1950s and into the 1970s, Lethbridge's downtown bustled with men's clothing stores including McGuire's, Gelfonds, Stan's Men's Wear with personable Remo Baceda, Buyrite, Albert's operated by Dan Shapiro's father, Leo Singer's, Christie Grants with Herb Shector, and a store operated by Sam Roskin. In a city full of quality clothiers, Reno gained a reputation for being among the best. Not bad for the son of a coal miner.

Reno was born in Coalhurst in 1926 and lived in the booming mining community until the disastrous explosion of Dec. 9, 1935, when 16 miners met their deaths in the bowels of the mine.

"We lived a block from the mine, where my dad (John Lizzi) was a coal miner. He wasn't hurt in the explosion, but I can sort of remember that disastrous day and the fact that just a year before fire had destroyed most of the main street in town. The day of the explosion it was cold and windy and there was a big sheet of loose metal high on the tipple. It was blowing and banging in the wind. It was very eerie. That was a scarey night. Back then Coalhurst had rows and rows of mine houses and a big ash pile right at the east end of the town."

After the explosion and the closing of the mine, Coalhurst's remaining miners left in droves, including the Lizzi family who moved to north Lethbridge. John Lizzi found work in the small Royal View Mine, in the Oldman River Valley. The Lizzi's lived on 7th Avenue North and Reno attended St. Basil's School, through Grade 8. He then headed south across the tracks to St. Pat's, where the County of Lethbridge building now stands.

He'd walk to and from school at lunchtime as well as before and after school.

"In the winter we'd be all wrapped up and in overalls and we'd cut across the railroad tracks, hit 13th Street and then head over to the school," Reno said.

At age 17 he joined the army. The war in Europe was winding down and he, like many other young men, was being honed for the Japanese theatre of action when the war in the Pacific ended.

Herald Photo
Avid baseball fan Reno Lizzi

46

"I did wind up working for the big Concentration Camp in north Lethbridge, taking prisoners of war from the camp to a camp in Magrath," Reno said. "At Magrath the guys would work on farms in the area. I'd take guys out to the Ernie Biggs farm, a couple of miles west and north of Magrath. We were armed, of course, but the guys we were guarding were mainly young German kids. Many of them were movie buffs and I'd get the movie magazines of the era for them to read."

Reno wasn't in any fighting but he, like so many others, was personally touched by the war. At Christmas time, in 1943, he received a letter from his best friend, Hank Oberg. The letter arrived a week after Oberg had been killed in action in Europe. It left a lasting mark.

After the war Reno worked with Trans Canada Airlines for a while, in 1947, before turning to the clothing business. In 1954 he married Joyce and the Lizzi's had five children: Curt, Gail, Diane, Mark and Brenda.

Reno, a devoted sports fan, left an indelible mark on Lethbridge. For years he was a key up-front and also behind-the-scenes worker with the annual Kinsmen Sportsmen's Dinner. But beyond the dinner, baseball fans in Lethbridge, due in large part to Reno's work, enjoyed the opportunity to watch, and come to know, some of the sport's top players through the years.

In 1975 he was the main man behind the scenes who helped bring in the Pioneer Baseball League and the fledgling Montreal Expo rookies. Among those rookies was now baseball Hall of Famer, Andre Dawson. Then, from 1977 to 1981, the Los Angeles Dodgers had their rookie team based in Lethbridge.

"I had tried to get the Blue Jays - between the Expos and the Dodgers - but they were just going into the Major Leagues and were uncertain where they wanted to set up," said Reno. Instead, the Dodgers came to town, and with them players like Steve Sax, Greg Brock, Mike Marshall, Candy Maldanado, Gary LaRocque and Ron Kittle, and former Major Leaguers who went into coaching like Jim Lefevbre, Ron Peronnoski, Johnny Roseboro, Larry Sherry and Chico Fernandez. "Those were good times," Reno said with a wistful smile.

Through his experience with Major League Baseball on a local level, Reno was able to go on and enjoy the "Show" itself, taking in games, playoff action and World Series games. It was a dream come true for the former dapper Lethbridge haberdasher.

In the early days of the Pioneer League in Lethbridge, players were just on the verge of the boom years of super contracts, the era of the multi-million-dollar utility man still in the future. "Today, I think sports have gone crazy," said Reno. "There's too much money for the athletes and too much is needed to set up franchises. There's also too much spread between the haves and the have nots."

Reno's association with the Kinsmen began when he was asked by Warren Frache to join the club. "I went to work with the dinner committee right away. I really loved what I was doing."

But Reno wasn't one to dwell on the past. He kept few mementoes from the baseball teams and the Kinsmen banquet days. "It is a part of my life that has passed," he said.

Featured speakers and major sports stars coming all the way to Lethbridge from major league cities, charged a mere $300 to $500. These celebrities included sports immortals like Jesse Owens, Sandy Koufax, Sayers, Whitey Ford, Jim Brown, Rocky Marciano and even comedian Rich Little. "Rich Little was at the peak of his career and that was the biggest dinner the Kinsmen ever put on, well over 2,200 people," said Reno.

Naturally, through the 20-year history of the banquet, not all athletes showed up. Willie Mays was all signed and sealed, but undelivered. In his backing out, Reno recovered well, bringing in baseball great Jimmy Pearsall.

Sugar Ray Robinson was also a no-show and Rev. Bob Richards, the Olympian, didn't make it either. But dozens of other did, including George Chuvalo, Canada's legendary heavyweight champion, still sporting the bruises from his fight with ex-world champion Floyd Patterson just a few days earlier.

The biggest name in football, Jim Brown, attended the Kinsmen Dinner. "Jimmy Brown was a very impressive man," said Reno. "He was the biggest man I ever saw, from shoulders to waist. He wore a 52 suit coat, with a 34 waist." (Who else but a haberdasher would notice that?)

Los Angeles Dodgers owner Peter O'Mally was never a guest, but he did attend the banquet on one occasion, escorting the Dodgers' immortal catcher, Roy Campenella.

"I wanted to get Yogi Berra, the Yankee catcher, but Joe Garagiola told me Yogi just didn't like to travel. We tried, but we finally gave up on him. We did try for the Packers' Bart Starr too because we'd been told he was a fantastic speaker, but it just didn't happen. It was always tough to get NHL players because the season was on and we'd only get retired or injured players. But all in all, we pretty much got whoever we went after. We'd meet, decide who we wanted and then start making the calls."

Being an outstanding athlete doesn't mean you will be a great, or even good, public speaker. But, for the most part, the Kinsmen came up lucky as evidenced by the outstanding job of men like Jake LaMotta, the former world middleweight champion.

"Jerry Kramer, the great pulling guard from the Green Bay Packers was a good speaker," said Lizzi. "He was a good guest, period." Sometime after the banquet visit, Kramer and some buddies were hunting in the Elko, B.C. area. Unfortunately one of the men in the group was accidentally shot. Kramer immediately phoned Reno. The Kinsmen arranged for Lethbridge Dr. Frank Christie to look after the situation, and all ended well.

With very few exceptions, if an athlete achieved any renown at all between 1954 and 1973, he was a featured guest of the Lethbridge Kinsmen Sportsmen's Dinner.

The Kinsmen Club, year after year, brought the best of the best to this city. Jesse Owens, the man who humbled

Those at the 1956 banquet, will never forget past world heavyweight champion Rocky Marciano's opening remarks to the huge crowd, which he used to qualify himself as a speaker: "I'm not pretty, I can't give a speech very well, and I'm not elegant . . . but I'll fight any son of a bitch in the house!"

Hitler; Rocky Marciano, the only man to retire as undefeated world heavyweight champion; the great middleweight champion Jimmy McLarnin; and Sandy Koufax, arguably the best left-hander in baseball history, were among the Kinsmen guests. Wrestlers like Gene Kiniski; Bobby Unser the Indy 500 winner; world champion cowboys like Kenny McLean and Casey Tibbs; the NHL's great Jacques Plante; and entertainer Dave Broadfoot were also members of the long, impressive list.

Behind the scenes, year after year was Reno. "We tried to touch all sports, we went after everyone because each sport brought in its followers," said Reno. "What scared me every year, was once an athlete said yes he'd come, that someone else would come along on our date and offer him more money. A lot would come here and go straight on to New York for a dinner there."

John Wichers did all of the catering, first through the El Rancho when he was there, and then with Sven Erickson's Family Restaurant. He was Erickson's head man from the El Rancho Coffee Shop Days and through to the Family Restaurant era. Reno had great praise for Wichers, who was always prepared to lay on 40 to 50 last-minute plates if there was a sudden rush at the door the night of the dinner. "He'd serve 1,000 to 2,000 people and the meals were always good, and hot," said Reno. "He was a major part of the success of the banquet as far as I'm concerned, especially with the two dinners I chaired." Reno said many

Rocky Marciano and Roy Campanella

other people cooperated as well. The airlines people were able to offer a free pass or two, and organizations like the NHL, the Calgary Stampeders, and the Canadian Professional Rodeo Association helped out by sending athletes to the dinner. "We always covered our expenses," said Reno.

Herald Photo

Kinsmen Bob Rose, 1960 dinner chairman, and Tom Hunt check out Archie Moore's muscles

"The booze people were good too. We always had our press conferences at the Sick's Brewery, in the Snake Room. The guys selling the hard stuff were always knocking at our doors. The Snake Room was great, it was one-on-one down there, and like the banquet it was strictly stag. We tried to bring in the guys the night before and we'd have a banquet upstairs at the Exhibition Pavilion for the Kinsmen, their wives and special guests, and that's the only time the ladies were allowed."

Reno said key figures behind the beginning of the dinner included Don Pilling and Hugh Buchanan of The Herald, and Kinsmen like Harold Brown, Bus Murdoch and Don Wilson.

"The dinners were always the end of January or first of February. When I became involved I'd always try to guess who the World Series MVP would be, *before the Series,* and go after the player before they became wanted by everyone. The first one I guessed right was Whitey Ford. I guessed with Tom Tresh too.

"Tresh was here in 1965 and forgot to pack a necktie, so I took him downtown to our store (Black's Men's Wear), but we had to park a block or so away. As we were walking we passed two Hutterite men, they turned and said, 'Hey, you're Tom Tresh!' Tom was as fascinated as they were, he'd never seen Hutterites before."

Of all the dozens and dozens of men who graced the head table

Herald Photo

Jake LaMotta was easily one of the best speakers the Kinsmen ever had

through the years, Reno selected Dr. Michael J. Pecarovich as the finest speaker. Pecarovich, who died just a month or so after attending the Lethbridge banquet, was from California and often talked to sports teams and college crowds. "The man was one of the most motivational speakers I've ever heard," said Reno. "He kept our entire crowd in its seats, no one moved, no one got up and left."

Reno used to work with other sportsmen dinner groups, in Billings, Montana and Spokane, and the three would exchange names and ideas. That's where he learned of Pecarovich. Reno knew what he was getting and arranged for the speaker to come into town a few days early to speak at the LCI, Winston Churchill and Catholic Central High Schools. "He kept every kids' attention and he did the same thing again with the 1,500 at the dinner.

"CJOC Radio used to tape the banquet and play it the following Sunday. I had two or three tapes of the speech Pecarovich made and I sent one of them down to him. I'm glad I did, because, after he died, I phoned his wife to express my condolences and she thanked me for the tape. She said she had never heard him speak before."

Those who heard him that night will tell you former world middleweight boxing champion Jake LaMotta was among the finest after-dinner speakers to be found.

Once he left the ring Jake, subject of the Academy Award-wining movie *Raging Bull,* took a few years "to find himself" before moving into acting, TV commercials, guest appearances and after-dinner speaking.

LaMotta was a head-table guest at the 1968 version of the Dinner, and he wowed them.

Reno, the dinner chairman, had been told LaMotta would be the hit of the show. And he was.

"Jake flew into Lethbridge from New York and he arrived without a suitcase," Reno said with a laugh. "When I asked him why, he said, 'Ain't they got stores here?' We had put him up at the Park Plaza and the next morning, about 10 a.m., I went over and commented on what a beautiful morning it was. He laughed at me and said, 'I don't know about that. This is ridiculous, this is the first time I've ever been up this early.' That was Jake, all weekend long, one line after the other."

Jake LaMotta was born of Italian-Jewish parents July 10, 1921 in New York City. Like most kids growing up in that huge metropolis he was wild, and as a result spent some time in reform school.

By the time 1941 rolled around, Jake found himself in the professional fight business. Jake's ways in the ring were as rough as they had been out of the ring. Dubbed The Bronx Bull, Jake was soon earning top money and fighting the best the fistic world had to offer at the time.

Jake shocked the boxing world when he became the first man to beat Sugar Ray Robinson. In all, Jake and Robinson battled six times. Robinson won five of these - "I fought Sugar Ray so many times, I think I caught diabetes," LaMotta claimed. Jake feels he won three of the six bouts, but was robbed by bad decisions. Times were good for Jake, then the roof caved in.

In 1947, LaMotta was of offered a title shot - if. The "if"? Jake was to throw a fight with Billy Fox. In the fourth round of their bout Billy Fox kayoed Jake. An investigation was held and LaMotta was suspended for six months and fined $500. June 14 and 15, 1960, in front of the Kefauver Subcommittee on Antitrust and Monopoly which was investigating the boxing game, Jake admitted he had taken a "dive."

On June 16, 1949, LaMotta got his title shot. He took only 10 rounds to dispose of French idol Marcel Cerdan and take away his middleweight

Herald Photo
Reno Lizzi and Jake LaMotta

crown. Jake LaMotta was on top. He defended his title twice before taking on Ray Robinson. The fight was stopped in the 13th round with Jake draped helplessly over the ropes. It was one fight he didn't claim was a bad decision.

At the 1968 Dinner he asked me how long the committee wanted him to talk, and if he was the wind-up speaker. I told him "no," umpire Jocko Conlon was the wind-up guy and called Reno over to find out how long LaMotta should talk. Based on what we all saw and heard in the Snake Room, LaMotta was a man who could barely finish a sentence. Reno told him to speak the shortest time reasonable, just 20 minutes, and walked away.

LaMotta looked at me and said, "Conlon eh? I'll murder da bum!" And he did. Ten minutes into Conlon's speech the huge crowd was still laughing at, and retelling, LaMotta jokes. As for the time element, he opened his coat and showed us three cigars. "I got one cigar for 20 minutes, one for 40 and one for an hour."

Gene Kiniski, a former guard at the provincial jail in Lethbridge who went on to become the world wrestling champion, was another favourite of Reno's. What reveals Kiniski's character was the fact he flew all day Saturday - he had been wrestling in the east - to be in Lethbridge for the banquet that night. The trip included his renting a car in Calgary and driving down. Besides all this, and the fact he was a great guest, Kiniski didn't charge the Kinsmen a penny.

If you ever wanted to get Reno kind of choked up, you'd have to touch on the guest who held the fondest memories for Reno, baseball broadcaster Joe Garagiola. He and Joe - who was a catcher during his playing career before he became a top sportscaster - remained lifelong friends as a result of Joe's appearance at the dinner.

"Joe was as nice a man as we ever had at the dinner," said Reno. "He always felt his stories could be told anywhere, to anyone. He's one nice guy. His stories about himself and about baseball are the funniest you'll ever hear. They're classics." Reno visited with Garagiola many times since that 1962 dinner, including at baseball's all-star game when it was in Toronto.

Henry Viney was the Kinsmen's first choice for an emcee when the banquet first began, and he added a great touch with his white dinner jacket and cigar, said Reno.

"Rich Little and Dave Broadfoot were good speakers - they did their acts actually," said Reno. "But really, I think they took a little something away from the dinner. They weren't in sports, but both were at their peak at the time they came here and they drew lots of people."

When he sat down and started to compile a list of Kinsmen Sportsmen Dinner guests, Don Pilling was astounded. Despite being one of the founders of the illustrious banquet, which held sway in the city from 1954 through 1973, the former Lethbridge Herald Sports Editor and later Managing Editor, was still startled at the star-status of the athletes who found their way to this city for a winter weekend each year.

Don Pilling brought a solid sports background to his role in the Kinsmen Sportsmen Dinners. Besides being the Sports Editor of The Lethbridge Herald, and later Managing Editor, he was an athlete in his youth and was on hand for a few of sports' most memorable moments.

He was born in Oregon, but moved to Lethbridge with his family while still a youngster. His father, Frank Pilling, was an international calibre trap-shooting champion and was also a professional wrestling champion, in an era when wrestling was considered a legitimate sport. Don turned his talents to hockey and fastball as a young man, playing on the elite junior level with the Lethbridge Native Sons.

His fastball career included a stint with the 1946 Western Canadian Junior Champions, the Lethbridge Dodgers. Bill Kucheran managed the team and players included another soon-to-be Herald writer Ron Watmough, as well as others like Francis Wright, "Boomer" Rodzinyak, Rocky Robinson, Eddie Foychuk and George Spoulos.

Don began writing sports for The Herald when his neighbour, Harold Long, Managing Editor of

The Herald at the time, asked the young teen to cover a few events during the Second World War. By 1949, Pilling was in the business full bore, as Sports Editor of The Lethbridge Herald. His coverage and interest went beyond the boundaries of southern Alberta. Don was in Vancouver in 1954 for the British Empire Games, when Roger Bannister beat John Landy in the Miracle Mile, the first time two men ever ran the mile in under four minutes in the same race. In 1951 he also watched Bobby Thompson hit the home run "heard around the baseball world" to lead the New York Giants past the Brooklyn Dodgers for the right to head into the World Series. Of course, he stayed to watch the Yankees beat the Giants in the Series. In the stands with Pilling were other area sports fans, Ken Ringland and Henry Viney of Lethbridge and Joe Kubik of Blairmore. They had been lucky enough to arrive for the World Series a few days early, enabling them to catch the Giants-Dodgers playoff game. The Giants capped off a comeback from 15 and a half games back to win the pennant in the old Polo Grounds in New York with Thompson's home run.

"The great Jackie Robinson was the second baseman for the Dodgers then, and as soon as Thompson hit the ball, Robinson drop kicked his glove into the Dodgers' dugout," Don said. "I'll never forget that."

Before the Series' opener, Leo Durocher the fiery Giant manager held a press conference. Among the reporters in the front row was Viney and his ever-present cigar. The smoke filled the

Photo Courtesy Galt Archives
Henry Viney

air and seemed to blow directly towards Durocher. Leo the Lip wheeled, facing the portly radio broadcaster and told him to either put the cigar out, or leave. "Henry took one last puff, blew out the smoke, turned and left," Pilling said with a laugh.

Several years later, Henry was emceeing the Kinsmen Dinner in Lethbridge, and was at a reception being held at Ringland's home. Viney, decked in his white dinner jacket, was standing at the base of the stairs, smoking his cigar when Ringland escorted Durocher, a head table guest for the fifth annual dinner, into the room.

"Durocher was on the second step when he looked down and saw Henry," Don recalled. "He looked at Henry and said, `for heaven's sake, don't tell me you're still smoking those stinking things!' It was seven years later, in Lethbridge, Alberta, for goodness sakes . . . a long way from Yankee Stadium! It was amazing, because it was the first time Durocher had seen Henry since the incident at the press conference. It was the first time I ever saw Henry speechless."

Don was the master of ceremonies for the 15th dinner in 1968. He always had a reputation for being a perfectionist and wanted nothing less than the perfect dinner. "Reno was the one who talked me into it. I fretted and stewed about it, I'll tell you I did."

The afternoon, before virtually each and every dinner, the Kinsmen held a press conference downstairs in the main office of the Sick's Lethbridge Brewery, in the Snake Room. It was there Pilling first met Jake LaMotta, former world middleweight boxing champion for the first time. LaMotta was rough around the edges, to say the least and he sounded like anything but a good speaker. For the smooth, straight-laced Pilling it looked like a disaster in the making. Pilling was shaken, as was Lizzi, the dinner chairman. After the conference, Pilling went home and laid down for a hour or so rest before the big banquet and his demanding role as emcee. He thought of LaMotta and impending disaster later that night.

"All I could think was, `oh boy, why me?' At the banquet Jake was seated right next to me and was set to be the second last speaker. I'll never forget what happened as long as I live. As he got up to speak, he leaned over to me and said, `don't worry kid, everything is under control.' It was. LaMotta gave one of the best speeches I've ever heard. Afterwards, he told me he had paid a Hollywood scriptwriter $15,000 to write him three speeches, and he'd given them dozens of times. He knew they were good. It was marvellous."

The dinner was what Don wanted - perfection - though it must be said, LaMotta was so good he simply buried the featured speaker who followed him, baseball umpire Jocko Conlan.

Herald Photo

Don Pilling

The next morning LaMotta was heading back to New York, in a strong Lethbridge wind, leaving from the tiny Lethbridge airport. A Piper Cub was front and centre on the runway, literally being held down in the wind by two men, as LaMotta and company arrived. Someone told the ex-champ that was the plane for him, to carry him to Calgary. The look on LaMotta's face was priceless, said Pilling.

Don also remembered undefeated world heavyweight boxing champion Rocky Marciano. He spoke fondly of the two-fisted slugger, who to this day is still the only heavyweight champion to retire undefeated, at 49-0, with 46 wins by knockout. There was a special private moment as Don and the champ ate a noon meal at the Park Plaza, and Don recalled Marciano signing two of the coffee shop's menus for two admiring patrons.

Pilling also remembered Marciano's favourite line: "If you ask me if I could beat Ali (Muhammad Ali, then world heavyweight champion) and I said yes . . . then I'd be a braggart. But, if I said 'no' . . . then I'd be a liar."

Class is a word associated with only a few top-calibre athletes. But being a star in a sport does not necessarily make you a class act as a human being, something the Kinsmen Sportsmen's Dinner people discovered through the years.

They also discovered there were a lot of classy people out there. Such was the case with Jesse Owens. Not only was the 1936 Olympic star a world-renowned athlete, he was also the epitome of class. "I have great memories of Jesse Owens," Don said concerning the 1969 Kinsmen Dinner guest. "I was honoured to be able to spend an evening with him and have supper with him and Ken Reardon (Montreal Canadien star) at the Park Plaza. Owens was a classy person.

"As well, I can't say enough about Al Kaline (Detroit Tigers and a 1957 guest). He too was a terrific guy. And Jim Coleman (newspaper sports columnist and 1954 and 1955 guest), well, you couldn't meet a finer guy and you couldn't find a finer sports writer."

Don's list of classy people goes on, and

includes Bud Grant, the former Winnipeg Blue Bomber star, and Minnesota Viking head coach, as well as Les Lear, Sparky Anderson and Sam Etchevery. Don and Etchevery, the Montreal Alouettes quarterback and a dinner guest in 1954 and 1955, became friends and it was Etchevery to whom Pilling turned when a scheduled guest pulled out at the last minute. A phone call to Montreal was returned in short order and Etchevery had baseball's Sparky Anderson, manager of the Cincinnati Reds and later Detroit Tigers, lined up and ready to come to Lethbridge.

Sparky Anderson, who was in Montreal for a sports banquet at the time on a Friday night, flew to Lethbridge for Saturday's dinner, and was back on the plane, headed for New York and a Sunday banquet. Another class act.

Many of the guests came into Lethbridge and took part in other activities besides the dinner itself. There were private dinners, gatherings, press conferences, TV dates and even school visits, speaking to the students, as Dr. Michael J. Pecarovich did in 1965.

"At of the early dinners we had a junior hockey game in the old arena on a Friday night, and there was Bob Feller, a baseball Hall of Famer, at centre ice," said Pilling. "He was in his shirt sleeves, with baseball in hand, pitching to Frankie Anderson of the Edmonton Eskimos, with a hockey stick in his hand, and Gus Kyle, another football player, was umping. It absolutely brought the house down."

Pilling said the NHL was always well represented with former greats, and he marveled at the fact men like Cyclone Taylor and Lester Patrick were in Lethbridge together. Each year brought special stars, new stresses, different stories and after 20 years, dozens of special memories and individual memories for the thousands of fans who attended.

For Don Pilling, the most memorable moment of all came in 1966. "I was fortunate enough to attend the World Series in 1952 when the Brooklyn Dodgers lost to the Yankees. While there I met, among others, Jackie Robinson and Roy Campenella. Campy was a fun-loving guy."

Herald File Photo
Jim Coleman

But, in 1954, Campenella was paralyzed in a car crash, to spend the rest of his days in a wheelchair. More than a decade later the great Dodger catcher and Baseball Hall of Famer was part of the 1966 Kinsmen Sportsmen's Dinner.

"He had a room at the El Rancho and I went over and talked with him. I told him how I'd met him at Ebbetts Field, at the Series, and we talked about those days. He was a classy man. When they wheeled him out onto the stage for the dinner that night . . . well, what a moving moment that was."

My Personal look

For me the Kinsmen Sportsmen Dinners were a chance for a naive young northsider to walk among the elite. I started work at The Lethbridge Herald in 1958, as a printer at age 15. My first treat was making up the sports pages with guys like Don Pilling and Don Maclean. Each January, and later February, those pages included galley after galley of lead type focusing on the Kinsmen Dinner.

The two Dons would talk of their personal experiences with the super stars the dinner attracted. Guys I worked with, like Frank Sherman and Bill Kennedy had stories of the banquets. I couldn't go, you had to be 21, and I was a young mid-teen.

Occasionally one of the sporting greats showed up at The Herald, and you could get a glimpse of them. As well, they'd appear in public. I recall Sam Etchevery, the Montreal quarterback, and Bob Feller of the Cleveland Indians, throwing footballs and baseballs on 5th Street one day when I was exiting the old Roxy Theatre.

Friends of our family included George and Elzeda Wylie, who owned Wylie's Tartan Shop on 5th Street. While in town world light-heavyweight champion Archie Moore, and his wife, visited the shop and Moore bought a wool curling sweater. I was in the store at the time and met the great champion! Moore later told folks he purchased a hand-knitted sweater at "Willy's Tar-Tan Shop."

Herald photographers like Orville Brunelle,

Ken Sakamoto and Elwood Ferguson also gave me special prints of the stars, which I'd have autographed when possible.

My real break came when Don Pilling told me I could interview some of the guests, the cowboys and the boxers, and he arranged with Jack McCrea, who owned the Ad-Viser, for me to do some writing for the weekly paper. Those moves opened huge doors for me – I got to attend the press conferences in the Brewery Snake Room. There I was, interviewing people like Moore, Jake LaMotta, Sam Jones of the Boston Celtics, cowboys like Kenny MacLean, Winston Bruce, Dick Havens, Harold Mandeville and old schoolmate Malcolm Jones.

Herald Phoro
Archie Moore

Don allowed me, as time passed, to write stories for The Herald and I did interviews with world boxing champs Joey Giardello, Carmen Basilio, Jake LaMotta and also Jerry Quarry. I was able to spend a couple of hours in a room with super stars like Gayle Sayers (whom Pat Sullivan interviewed), Ferguson Jenkins, Rocky Marciano, Roman Gabriel and Ted Peck - remember the TV fisherman?

But the most memorable moment for me came in a room in the Park Plaza, where the immortal Jesse Owens lay across his bed and allowed a mere kid to interview him. That moment, in 1969, was shared with old Herald buddy Jock Mulgrew. To this day, on my office wall, I still have the autographed Polaroid I took of Jesse Owens, laying across his motel room bed reading the Ad-Viser.

Owens, voted in 1990 as the Champion of the Century, talked about how track had been his life and after his career ended he made some extra cash racing Thoroughbreds over 100 metres, with a 10-yard head start. He said the key

Garry Allison Photo
Jessee Owens at the Park Plaza

to winning was the starter always fired the gun next to the horse, which would rear up, giving Owens an even bigger head start. "Also, I never raced a Quarter horse," he said with a laugh about the horses known for their early burst of speed.

Owens also said he loved hockey, the Chicago Blackhawks in particular, but for many years, even after his Olympic fame, he had to sit in the upper section, on the steps, because of his colour.

At the same dinner I was in heavyweight boxer Jerry Quarry's room and had a photo taken with him. I was saddened some years later when Quarry died, virtually a punch-drunk, speechless shell of the vibrant person I had visited with at the Park Plaza.

The Snake Room was a great place, with great food, and the whole affair was hosted by Spike Martell. It was a super pre-dinner bash. Then came the banquet. (For years my ticket was paid for by Jack McCrea and later by The Herald.) But things didn't end there. There was always the trip to the El Rancho and the roaming room-to-room parties with some of the super stars hanging around. Not all presented lily-white fronts.

The Snake Room also included another old northsider, Brent Seely, later to become head honcho at CJOC. We had both survived "Sam" Gaudette's Grade 9 class at Wilson Junior High and now we were walking in tall cotton. Another young full-time sportswriter at The Herald at the time was Pat "Sully" Sullivan, who got to do the big guys, like Gayle Sayers, because he was on-staff on a regular basis.

Henry Viney was often around as well and he always talked with me, calling me "kid." He'd always ask me about my Granddad and my Dad. Henry and my grandfather, Robert Allison, a bartender at the old Lethbridge Hotel, had been good friends. Reno Lizzi, the only two-time dinner chairman (in 1963 and 1968) treated me as if I was important, and helped line up an interview room for me – and the real reporters of course – in the main office above the Snake Room.

I remember some great moments, like meeting Bob Uecker and Dandy Don Meredith when they were signing into the Park Plaza, or Johnny Bower of the Maple Leafs talking about how they had to teach Lanny Macdonald to skate when he became a Leaf. I remember Lethbridge's Eddie Ferenz bringing in a tall cool gin for boxer Joey Giardello during our interview.

I remember looking at Sam Jones, at 6-foot-7, and realizing he was a "short" guard in the NBA. While at the Snake Room bash for the 17th dinner in 1970 - once again in there under somewhat false pretenses - I decided to chat with Sam Jones of the Boston Celtics, a friendly, likeable guy. This is short, I thought?

I asked him to pick his all-time NBA all-star team. "Bill Russell, Elgin Baylor, Bob Petit, Oscar Robertson and Jerry West, (remember this is in the early 1970s) that's my all-star team," he said, peering down at me. "They are all great men and also great basketball players."

I asked Jones to compare Wilt Chamberlain - whom I would later meet and sit beside at the Commonwealth Games in 1978 in Edmonton - and Bill Russell. "If you're looking for a top rebounder and scorer, Wilt is your man. If it's a defensive expert, a winner - and that's important - and an unselfish man, then you choose Russell."

Naturally there were people I wanted to meet who never made it, like Sugar Ray Robinson. I also wanted to interview Floyd Patterson and Ingemar Johanson.

Once again Don Pilling figures in here with my "want tos". He had arranged for me to meet Ingomar Johansson, at the old Marquis Hotel. I had met and interviewed George Chuvalo at the dinner and many times since. But I always wanted to meet the man who beat Patterson and Eddie Machen with his "tunder and lightning." Patterson, of course came back and won the title in a re-match.

For Ingemar, Don came into the composing room at The Herald and told me Ingo had secretly checked into the Marquis and if I wanted I could run down there and grab an interview with him. Off I went. But the heavyweight champion had just left for Glacier National Park. He was filming a war movie there with Allan Ladd.

Pilling suggested I follow the champion there, which I did. They were filming all right, and the Logan Pass was closed off, though our Herald photographer got through. I never did see Ingomar and Don got a great chuckle out of that. "That's a reporter's life," he laughed.

One of the sidelights of the Kinsmen banquet which was really an important ingredient, though few people paid great attention to their creators, was the art work of Arian Pontarollo and Darcy Rickard of The Herald. They did pre-banquet sketches and did programs for the dinner. The huge drawings out front for some of the head tables were special features, done by Arnie Weir of Hook Signs. Reno said that Jack Foster bought some of those huge drawings for his club in Great Falls - all autographed, of course!

Even while the dinners were taking place, the people of southern Alberta really didn't realize just how lucky we were. The greatest athletes in the world were brought to our small prairie city, and we were able to see them, hear them and for the really lucky ones, meet them.

It is an era I'll never forget.

Following is a list, as near as can be complied, of all the Kinsmen Sportsmen Dinners, their location, the chairmen, masters of ceremonies, guests and the city's athletes and sportsmen of the year, a major acknowledgment the Kinsmen performed during most banquets:

First
Jan. 15, 1954
Marquis Hotel
Dinner Chairman - Jim Crane
MC - Henry Viney
Dinner Guests - Jim Coleman, sports columnist; Al Ritchie, Regina sportsman and coach; Normie Kwong and Rollie Miles, Edmonton Eskimos; Sam Etchevery, Montreal Alouettes, George Vogan and Harper Parry of the Western Junior Hockey League.

Lethbridge Sports Hall of Fame
Henry Viney

2nd Annual
Jan. 14, 1955
Marquis Hotel
Dinner Chairman - Les Paton
MC - Henry Viney
Dinner Guests - Sam Etchevery, Montreal Alouettes; Rollie Miles and Normie Kwong of the Edmonton Eskimos; Frank Boucher, GM of the New York Rangers; Doug Smith, sports commentator; Jim Coleman, sports columnist; Les Lear, Calgary Stampeder coach; Al Ritchie, Regina sportsman.
Athlete of the Year - Eddie Schwartz, golf
Sportsman Honouree - Ed Bruchet

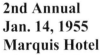

Courtesy Galt Archives
Eddie Schwartz

3rd Annual
Jan. 13, 1956
Civic Sports Centre
Dinner Chairman - Gordon Spackman
MC - Henry Viney
Dinner Guests - Bob Feller, Cleveland Indians; Normie Kwong, Edmonton Eskimos; Frankie Anderson, Edmonton Eskimos; Glen Gorbous, Philadelphia Phillies; Gordie Stutridge, Saskatchewan Roughriders; Sugarfoot Anderson, Calgary Stampeders; Tom Foley, sports commentator; Doug Smith, sports commentator.
Athlete of the Year - Johnny Vaselenak, baseball
Sportsman of the Year - Ken Ringland

Courtesy Galt Archives
Ken Ringland

4th Annual
Jan. 18, 1957
Civic Sports Centre
Dinner Chairman - Lou Lanier
MC - Doug Smith
Dinner Guests - Henry Viney, broadcaster; Al Kaline, Detroit Tigers; Gordon "Porky" Brown, Harry Langford and Dick Huffman, Calgary Stampeders; Frankie Anderson and Eagle Keys, and Don Getty of the Edmonton Eskimos; Jimmy McLarnin, boxing champion, Tom Foley, sportswriter.
Athlete of the Year - Harry Blacker, basketball
Sportsman of the Year - George Wesley

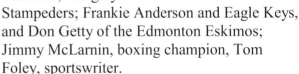

Don Getty

5th Annual
Jan. 24, 1958
Whoop-Up Guest Ranch (LCC Barn)
Dinner Chairman - Austin Whelihan
MC - Henry Viney
Dinner Guests - Leo Durocher, Major League Baseball manager; Henry Singer, Edmonton Eskimos; Herb Capozzi, B.C. Lions; Lew Burdett, Milwaukee Braves; Mervyn "Red" Dutton, Calgary Stampeders; Ted Tulley, Jackie Parker and Eagle Keys of the Edmonton Eskimos; John Ducey, minor league baseball.
Athlete of the Year - Jack Lilja, basketball
Sportsman of the Year - George McKillop

Courtesy Galt Archives
George McKillop

6th Annual
Jan. 23, 1959
Whoop-Up Guest
Ranch (LCC Barn)
Dinner Chairman - Tom
  Hunt
MC - Henry Viney
Dinner Guests - Vernon
  "Lefty" Gomez, New York
  Yankees; Bob Turley, New York Yankees;
  Yvonne Durrell, boxer; Lester Patrick and
  Cyclone Taylor, Hockey Hall of Fame; Al
  Ritchie and Father Athol Murray, well-known
  sportsmen; Bud Grant, NFL and CFL football
  coach; Harvey Wylie, Calgary Stampeders; Matt
  Baldwin, curling champion.
Athlete of the Year - Jim Furlong, football
  and basketball
Sportsman of the Year - Addie Donaldson

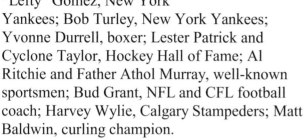
Jim Furlong

7th Annual
Jan. 23, 1960
Whoop-Up Guest
Ranch (LCC Barn)
Dinner Chairman - Bob Rose
MC - Henry Viney
Dinner Guests - Archie
  Moore, world champion
  boxer; Gil Hodges, Los
  Angles Dodgers; King
  Clancy, NHL Hall of
  Fame; Johnny Bright,
  Edmonton Eskimos; Doug Silverberg, amateur
  golf champion; Jim Finks and Bill McKenna of
  the Calgary Stampeders; Harold Brown,
  Broder's basketball.
Athlete of the Year - Rick Steadman,
  badminton
Sportsman of the Year - Dean Bennett

Lethbridge Sports Hall of Fame
Rick Steadman

8th Annual
Jan. 14, 1961
Whoop-Up Guest
Ranch (LCC Barn)
Dinner Chairman - Bill
  Bagshaw
MC - Henry Viney
Dinner Guests - Mel Allen,
  New York Yankee
  broadcaster; Elroy Face,
  Pittsburgh Pirates; Jackie

Courtesy Galt Archives
Sharon Smeed

Parker, Edmonton Eskimos; Ted Lindsay, Detroit
Red Wings; Keith Alexander, amateur golf
champion; Casey Tibbs, world champion saddle
bronc rider; Ernie Richardson, Canadian
champion curler; Gene Filipski, Calgary
Stampeders.
Athlete of the Year - Sharon Smeed, track and
  field
Sportsman of the Year - Stan Siwik

9th Annual
Feb. 3, 1962
Exhibition Pavilion
Dinner Chairman - Don
  MacLennan
MC - Henry Viney
Dinner Guests - Joe
  Garagiola, Major League
  Baseball, television
  broadcaster; Red Storey, NHL referee; Whitey
  Ford, New York Yankees; Gerry James, CFL
  and NHL; Tony Pajaczkowski and Larry
  Anderson, Calgary Stampeders; Hec Gervais,
  curling champion; Bob Wylie, amateur golf;
  Boyd Dowler, Green Bay Packers; Bob
  Hamilton, Broder's basketball coach; Winston
  Bruce, world saddle bronc champion.
Athlete of the Year - Lloyd Harris, Broder's
Sportsman of the Year - Alex Bennie

Whitey Ford

10th Annual
Jan. 26, 1963
Exhibition Pavilion
Dinner Chairman - Reno Lizzi
MC - Henry Viney
Dinner Guests - Jack Adams,
  Hockey Hall of Fame; Fred
  "Curly" Morrison, Chicago
  Bears of the NFL; Jimmy
  Brown, Cleveland Browns;
  Maury Wills, Los Angeles
  Dodgers; Spencer Harris, Manager Spokane
  Indians; Harvey Wylie and Jim Furlong,
  Calgary Stampeders; Kenny Ploen, Winnipeg
  Blue Bombers; Keith Hyland and Kenny
  McLean, rodeo cowboys; Phil Goyette,
  Montreal Canadiens; Dave "Sweeney" Shriner,
  Hockey Hall of Fame.
Athlete of the Year - Sam Kitagawa, weightlifter
Sportsman of the Year - Bill Rae

Courtesy Galt Archives
Bill Rae

57

11th Annual
Feb. 1, 1964
Exhibition Pavilion
Dinner Chairman - Andy Andreachuk
MC - Al McCann
Dinner Guests - Sandy Koufax, Los Angeles

Courtesy Galt Archives
Carol Hadford

Dodgers; Fresco Thompson, Dodger vice-president; Gene Fullmer, middleweight champion of the world and his manager Marv Jenson; Cletis Boyer, New York Yankees; Jerry Kramer, Green Bay Packers; Frank Selke, managing director Montreal Canadiens; Willie Fleming, B.C. Lions; Ted Peck, TV outdoor personality; Dick Havens, bronc rider; Don Luzzi, Calgary Stampeders; Wayne Harris, Calgary Stampeders.
Athlete of the Year Carol Hadford (Gemer), track and field
Sportsman of the Year - Frank Miles

12th Annual
Feb. 6, 1965
Exhibition Pavilion
Dinner Chairman - Ian Hamilton
MC - Henry Viney
Dinner Guests - Tom Brown, B.C. Lions; Tom Tresh, New York Yankees; Frank Ryan, Cleve- land Browns; Bobby Hewitson, NHL; Dr. Michael J. Pecarovich, motivational speaker; Jimmy Pearsall, Boston Red Sox; Lovell Coleman, Calgary

Courtesy Galt Archives
Yosh Senda

Stampeders; George Chuvalo, boxer; Tom Butterfield, rodeo; Marty Wood, world saddle bronc champion; J. Percy Page, Edmonton Grads coach.
Athlete of the Year - Bob Kasting, swimming
Sportsman of the Year - Yosh Senda

13th Annual
Feb. 5, 1966
Exhibition Pavilion
Dinner Chairman - Logan Tait
MC - Ernie Afaganis

Lethbridge Sports Hall of Fame
Syd Hall

Dinner Guests - Rich Little, comedian; Rocky Marciano, world heavyweight champion; Roy Campenella, Brooklyn Dodgers; Dutch Harrison, golfer; Harold Mandeville, rodeo; George Reed, Regina Roughriders; Gale Sayers, Chicago Bears; Jacques Plante, Montreal Canadiens.
Athlete of the Year- Joyce Meheden, track and field
Sportsman of the Year - Syd Hall

14th Annual
Feb. 4, 1967
Exhibition Pavilion
Chairman - Bill Van Buskirk
MC - Ernie Afaganis
Dinner Guests - Dave McNally, Baltimore Orioles; Gid Garstad, bull rider; Carmen Basilio, boxer; Brooks Robinson, Baltimore Orioles; Doug Barkley, Detroit Red

Courtesy Galt Archives
Bob Kasting

Wings; Hugh Campbell, Saskatchewan Roughriders; Marv Fleming, Green Bay Packers; Morris Frank, columnist; Paul Runyan, pro golfer; Dave Broadfoot, comedian.
Athlete of the Year - Bob Kasting, swimming
Sportsman of the Year - George Gemer

15th Annual
Feb. 3, 1968
Exhibition Pavilion
Chairman - Reno Lizzi
MC - Don Pilling
Dinner Guests - Ray Washburn, St. Louis Cardinals; Rocky Bridges, California Angels; Terry Evanshen, Calgary Stampeders; Gene Kiniski, wrestler; Ferguson Jenkins,

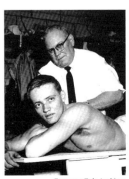
Courtesy Galt Archives
Darryl Knibbs &
Jack Kerr

Chicago Cubs; Brian O'Neill, NHL; Jake LaMotta, boxer; Jocko Conlan, Major League umpire.

Athlete of the Year - Darryl Knibbs, hockey
Sportsman of the Year - Jack Kerr, trainer

16th Annual
Feb. 4, 1969
Exhibition Pavilion
Chairman - Jim Frouws
MC - Ernie Afaganis

Courtesy Galt Archives
Alan Young

Dinner Guests - Jerry Quarry, boxer; Bobby Unser, Indy 500 champion; Tom Matte, Baltimore Colts; Rocky Rockabar, cowboy; Scotty Munro, hockey; Ken Reardon, Montreal Canadiens; Joe Hoerner, St, Louis Cardinals; Herm Harrison and Jim Furlong, Calgary Stampeders; Jesse Owens, Olympic star; Lloyd Mangrum, golfer.

Athlete of the Year - Alan Young, LCI football, and basketball
Sportsman of the Year - Alex Snowden

17th Annual
Jan. 31, 1970
Exhibition Pavilion
Chairman - Bob Parkyn
MC - Ernie Afaganis

Courtesy Galt Archives
Barb Horne

Dinner Guests - Jerry Keeling, Calgary Stampeders; Malcolm Jones, Canadian bareback bronc riding champion; Roman Gabriel, Los Angeles Rams; Bill "Dutch" Deelan, hockey referee; Sam Jones, Boston Celtics; Russ Jackson, Ottawa Rough Riders; Tommy Lasorda, LA Dodgers; Jerry Koosman, New York Mets; Tommy Richardson, U.S. sportscaster.

Athlete of the Year - Barb Horne
Sportsman of the Year - Don McLean

18th Annual
Feb. 6, 1971
Exhibition Pavilion
Chairman - Paul Rusznak
MC - Ernie Afaganis

Herald Photo
Stan Carmichael

Dinner Guests - Tom Gorman, umpire; Sparky Anderson, Cincinnati Reds/Detroit Tigers; Scotty Munro, hockey; Ron Lancaster, Saskatchewan Roughriders; Don Meredith, Dallas Cowboys; Duke Sims, Los Angeles Dodgers; Johnny Bower, Toronto Maple Leafs; Arnold Haraga, rodeo; Paul Richards, sportsman.

Athlete of the year - Randy Wolstoncroft
Sportsman of the Year - Stan Carmichael

19th Annual
Feb. 5, 1972
Exhibition Pavilion
Chairman - Bill Johnson
MC - Normie Kwong

Normie Kwong

Dinner Guests - Joey Giardello, boxer; Don Jonas, Winnipeg Blue Bombers; John Brockington, Green Bay Packers; Dolph Schayes, NBA; Bob Uecker, baseball, TV personality; Wayne Harris, Calgary Stampeders; Tom Bews, rodeo; Ron Hunt, Montreal Expos.

Athlete of the Year - Tim Tollestrup, basketball
Sportsman of the Year - Leo Harrold

20th Annual
and Final Banquet
Feb. 3, 1973
Exhibition Pavilion
Chairman - Dwight Jensen
MC - Henry Viney

Phil Illingworth

Dinner Guests - Joe Rudi, Oakland Athletics; Jim Pearsall, Boston Red Sox; John Ferguson, Montreal Canadiens; Mike Curtis, Baltimore Colts; John Helton, Calgary Stampeders.

Athlete of the Year - Phil Illingworth, judo
Sportsman of the Year - Gordon Hoselton

Native Legends

I have spent an inordinate amount of time on the Kainai and Piikani Nations through the years, covering a wide variety of sports and school events - and I enjoyed every minute of it. I've gathered together a collection of stories of some of the people I met and dealt with, some of them brief stories, others a lot longer. One, you may note is an Olympian from the United States, another an Olympian from eastern Canada. Such was the impression Alwyn Morris and Billy Mills made on me, I feel their stories are vital to the Indian community, and what it takes to succeed.

Many of these athletes have become life-long friends, while with others it was a one-time association. I still see many of these people from time to time. Some have passed on, others have gone on to greater things and a few have met with adversity.

These short stories portray all at the peak of their athletic careers.

Al Pard of the Piikani Nation and Robert Wells from the Kainai Nation set the standard for years to come in basketball when they played for the Lethbridge Community College Kodiaks in the late 1970s. Under coach Ben Brooks the pair were the first Indians to play on a college or university team in southern Alberta.

Al, a graduate of St. Michael's High School in Pincher Creek, was a superb outside shooter while Robert, from the St. Mary's Warriors off the Kainai, played guard for the Kodiaks.

I'm proud both these ball players found a place to live in Lethbridge in my mother-in-law's basement suite, one of the few homes that opened its doors to the two basketball stars.

Garry Allison Photo
Al Pard, superb basketball shooter in the late 1970s

In later years Al also made a name for himself as a successful Quarter horse trainer at the Rocky Mountain Turf Club in Lethbridge.

Ironically about 20 years later the two former teammates came together again, both working in key positions with the Kainai Corrections program in the new correctional centre on the reserve, just a little northeast of the Fire Hall at Standoff.

Al Pard also spent a term on council at Brocket and found the experience less than rewarding. No matter what changes he'd put forward "the vote was always 11-1," he said with a laugh.

In 1992, I was fortunate enough to meet Alwyn Morris, certainly a role model for Canada's young people, Native or otherwise. The pressure of being a role model seemed something this former Tom Longboat Award winner was comfortable with.

Alwyn, a Mohawk Indian from the Kahanawake Reserve near Montreal, was a gold and bronze medalist at the 1984 Olympics in Los Angeles in the kayak competition. He also earned a silver medal in 1982 and bronze in 1983 in the world kayak championships and was the Canadian K-1 champion from 1980 through 1985.

Alwyn was a member of three Canadian Olympic teams, nine world championship teams and was a colour commentator for the canoeing and kayaking events with CTV for the 1992 Olympic Games in Barcelona, Spain.

Alwyn has gone beyond sports. He has appeared on television shows like Beachcombers and Sesame Street, has appeared in television commercials and was the subject of a large, colourful Olympic poster, holding an eagle feather high above his head, along with his Olympic medals.

As a mid-teenager Alwyn was involved in the drug scene, using marijuana then hashish and mescaline. "I was certainly moving into the heavier stuff," he said as we spoke during his visit to the Kainai Nation. "But when I woke up lying in the street, being kicked by people I didn't know, I decided it was time to move away from drugs. It was easy for me to see both ends of the spectrum, so I just opened up and let the good things happen."

It was then he began to pursue his athletic career in earnest. His role model was his late grandfather Thomas Morris, who led by the things he said and did. Gerald Kezar, "a whiteman" who said to Morris, "come out and try paddling, you'll enjoy it," was the man who gave Alwyn his opportunity.

One of the things Alwyn is most proud of is the fact he earned his Olympic medals as a drug-free athlete. His initiation into the Olympic sports scene was a shocker when he saw athletes boosting their skills through drugs.

"When you see the side affects the drugs have on athletes you are racing against, you wonder to yourself, just what are they trying to do? I have too much pride in myself now to use drugs. I screwed up enough when I was 14 and 15 years old and the last thing I was going to do was screw up as an athlete."

Alwyn sees a Canada-wide system developing to help young Native athletes. He has a strong sense of the fact he was the only North American Indian competing in the 1984 Olympics. He also wants to see special schools established on reserves for top native athletes, places they could live throughout the school year and receive a top education combined with the best of coaching in their particular sport.

The schools would be very supportive, not like the old residential schools, he said. A foster parent system could be established where visiting athletes had a home away from home. The school could serve as a training centre for national teams, as international training sites and developed in such a way the program would pay for itself.

He found it very difficult to leave his reserve and seek higher training. But he knew he had to in order to achieve his goals. When he returned to

Garry Allison Photo

Alwyn Morris signs autographs for Kaiani fans

his reserve he found that the old friends who had ridiculed him for leaving to seek a better way, were mostly dead, through drug and alcohol abuse and related accidents. It was obvious who had the last laugh!

Taking up a challenge by a younger brother proved to be masterful move for Hank Bruised Head of the Kainai Nation. When his brother Gordie challenged him to take up steer riding, after Hank teased him about being bucked off, neither one could foresee that Hank would become the 2000 World Indian Rodeo Association bull riding champion, the youngest champion in the competition's history. And he'd only been riding bulls for two years.

Hank competed at 30 to 35 rodeos in 2000 on the Indian Rodeo Cowboys Association circuit, as well as the Chinook Amateur Rodeo Association, a few United States shows and at the World Indian Finals in Albuquerque, N.M. where he came away with the world championship.

"I also ride saddle broncs," he said at age 18, still basking in his championship. "I've learned it's a different rhythm and a different sense of balance than bull riding. It's harder than bull riding. Bulls are kind of addictive though. Once you get on and ride, you want to ride more and more."

Hank said you often can't see a bull's head when it is bucking so he concentrates on the hump, just in front of his bull rope. He can also feel the bull's movement with his lower body, and reacts to it unconsciously. "Your body just reacts, you don't have time to think about what to do," he said. "I focus on the basics of keeping my chin tucked, moving my feet and staying up on my rope. I just use a normal double wrap, sometimes called the suicide wrap. They call it that because if you buck off away from the wrap it won't unwrap and, well . . ."

Hank Bruised Head looked up to his Uncle

Byron, a tough all around hand who competed in three riding events and steer wrestling as well. "Byron taught me to ride bulls," said Hank. "The best thing he told me was if the bull doesn't buck, spur him; and if the bull is bucking and rank, spur him anyway."

A member of the Piikani Nation, Tyrone Potts took a different route to leaving his mark on the sports scene, along with setting a precedent with Canada's police force. For Tyrone it was the fulfilment of a dream, the achievement of a goal. Potts transferred from the RCMP detachment in Pincher Creek, where he worked for many years, and headed for Ottawa in 1991 where he began training to become part of the world famous RCMP Musical Ride.

Tyrone, a direct descendant of Northwest Mounted Police scout Jerry Potts, had been in the RCMP for six years, the last year as a regular constable. He, his late uncle Henry Potts and cousin Janet Potts all became RCMP constables at the same time after serving as special Native constables. Henry headed the Brocket sub-detachment, where Janet also worked. Another relative, cousin Stan Grier, was also an RCMP constable posted at Olds, Alberta.

"As far as I know there hasn't been a Native with the RCMP Musical Ride . . . but even if there has, I know am the first Blackfoot," said Tyrone in 2001. He entered training with Dennis Fraser, a Cree from Fort McMurray. The pair completed a five-week selection course in Ottawa in late 1991 and were selected for the next course.

"It was a tough course just to get into," Tyrone said. "There were about 600 applicants that year and from them they select 24 members to try out. Of that 24, 12 were chosen to go into the Musical Ride."

At completion of the course, Tyrone realized his dream, and was named a regular on the

Potts Family Photo

Tyrone Potts, first Blackfoot selected for the famous RCMP Musical ride

internationally acclaimed Musical Ride. Unlike many who have gone into the course, it was not Tyrone's first experience with horses. He grew up around horses and was a champion rodeo bronc rider, team roper and bull rider. Among his achievements while in the RCMP was winning various bull riding events as well as the Alberta RCMP bull riding title.

The initial five-week Musical Ride course was rigorous. He had to adapt from the western style of riding he grew up with to the English style used in the ride. Candidates would ride about three hours each day and spent the rest of the time acquainting themselves with the horses, cleaning stalls and caring for the big all-black Thoroughbred-Belgian cross horses.

"Because of my previous riding experience I was tested out a lot," Tyrone said. "I got a lot of rough horses, the type that bucked and stuff. But I never fell off. A lot there had never ridden before and it was a daily thing to see someone fall off. A few were even afraid of horses when they started, but everyone was greatly improved by the end."

Former Pincher Creek RCMP Detachment Staff-Sgt. Don Funk said Tyrone Potts had a long-standing interest in the Musical Ride and enjoyed a great love for horses through his life. Funk added, "A point I want to make is it was not a case of his being Native that saw him selected. He was selected on the interest and ability he displayed. He will be an excellent ambassador for Canada."

There are 36 members on the Musical Ride, 32 performing at any one time. The extras help cover for illness, time off and facilitate the 24-hour shifts set up. Their horses are never left alone. There are at least two members of the ride with the horses 24 hours a day.

"Rufus Goodstriker was really a mentor for me," said Max Gibb, a former B-track jockey and

Alberta and United States featherweight boxing champion. "I admired Rufus so much, he was quite a charismatic guy. I remember Rufus back when I was a young bush-track jockey and racing against his horses quite often. He had some of those young Blood jockeys up on those horses and it was quite a race riding against them."

Rufus maintained his passion for horse racing throughout his life and raced horses in almost every race meet in Alberta, Saskatchewan, British Columbia, and the northwestern United States at one time or another. He revelled in the number of wins, place and show finishes through the years with his top Quarter horses and Thoroughbreds, which he owned and trained for more than four decades.

Rufus also drove chuckwagons and had a lot of horses for his wagon and outriders, some of

which he'd often run on the bush tracks, and I'd have to ride against them," said Max. "At the rodeos Rufus would often be entered as a steer decorator and in between rodeo events he'd be saddling his race horses to run in a featured race.

Rufus was the only Indian to win the J.B. McDonald high-point award twice (1957-58) at the Calgary Stampede, presented to the top Indian

Photo Courtesy Galt Archives

**In 1953 Rufus Goodstriker formed a boxing team on the Kainai Reserve.
Back row, from left, Pat Brewer. Jim Wells, Rufus, Chris Mills and Frank Eagle Tail Feathers. Front row, from left, George Whiteman, Pat Eagle Tail Feathers, Norbert Fox, Gilbert Blackwater and Gilbert Mills.**

competitor. Besides rodeo, chuckwagon racing and horse racing, which he remained involved and interested in until his death, Rufus was a superb amateur and professional boxer. He was one of the foremost athletes the Kainai Nation ever produced.

Rufus played goal in hockey, for St. Mary's. He had never skated before, so with his first game they put him in goal. His fast hands and sharp eyes kept him in the game for years.

Max always felt Rufus was somewhat of a pied piper for the young people of the reserve, involving them in horse racing, rodeo and boxing. Rufus dedicated 20 years as Director of Cross Bell Youth Camp and Dude Ranch, building this haven on the Blood Indian Timber Limits in 1968.Not to be tied down to just a few interests, Rufus also appeared in a number of Hollywood film productions - including Running Brave, the story of Olympic champion Billy Mills, whose story appears in the section. Rufus enjoyed playing hockey; served as a RCMP Special Constable; Band Councilor and Head Chief. He was an Ambassador for Canada; Bundle holder; and served with many tribal spiritual societies. At his passing he was a herbalist/healer in the ways of traditional Blackfoot medicine.

Besides being a boxer, Rufus Goodstriker also trained and managed fighters, including Gus Calf Robe.

Gus fought in more than 100 amateur fights, winning the Golden Gloves and amateur titles many times in Alberta and Washington State, in the middleweight to light-heavyweight divisions. He also won the Canadian amateur championship and in 1962 had his biggest win right here at Exhibition Park in Lethbridge, taking the Western Canadian Light-heavyweight professional championship from Al Sparks of Winnipeg.

Along the way, Gus' brother Hugh encouraged and trained him, as did Emil Smallface Sr., Rufus and Stephen Fox. Gus was also instrumental in starting the Bull Horn Boxing Club along with Horace Red Crow, Rodney First Rider and Sugar Red Crow.

"When I started boxing (in the 1950s as a featherweight), the Kainai Nation, mainly under Rufus, had top boxers like Gus, Eddie First Rider, Frank Wolf Child, and earlier Charlie Smallface. There were also a great many other top young fighters," said Gibb. "I often found myself on the Alberta team as the only white kid, surrounded by all those great Blood boxers. Through boxing I saw Rufus in a different light than I did in horse racing, though he was still sending out tough reserve kids to compete against me."

Max remembered Gus as the greatest of the Kainai Nation fighters. In 1958 Gus was named the Golden Boy at the Alberta Golden Gloves. Gus went on to win Canadian and American titles as well and was the winner in that super battle with Al Sparks.

"You know, Rufus would put me in to spar with Gus later on in his career. I was a featherweight and Gus was a light-heavyweight and they had me sparring with Gus to help increase his speed. I could hit Gus as hard as I could, but Rufus never allowed Gus to unload on me."

Once Max began operating the Rocky Mountain Turf Club (1996) he would often see Rufus at the track, as a horse owner and a fan. Rufus is also enshrined on the RMTC Horsemen's Wall of Fame in the Royal Ascot Betting Parlour.

"The first few years with the RMTC were meaningful for me because Rufus would often come out to the races," said Max. "I'd see Rufus when he came out and we'd get together each time and re-live those good ol' days.

"His son-in-law (Godfrey Weasel Head) was training some of Rufus' horses and Godfrey still carries on a great family tradition at the RMTC track."

First, former Blood Chief Rufus Goodstriker left the scene and then Gus Calf Robe passed on. Both closed chapters on southern Alberta sports history books and both left a lasting impression.

One of the great show cases of amateur boxing in 1975 was the Canada Winter Games, spotlighting two Kainai battlers. But the Canada Winter Games boxing, an event co-chaired by Ozzie Stubbs and myself, with a very competent committee, was hit by a tragedy.

In order to involve other areas of southern Alberta the boxing had been split between Claresholm and the Exhibition Pavilion in Lethbridge.

During one of the cards at Claresholm the event featured two boxers from the Kainai Nation, Hugh Calf Robe and Alvin Mills, both part of the Alberta team. And while it should have been the best of times for the two boys, it turned out to be the worst for young Calf Robe in particular.

Returning home after watching their son box in Claresholm, Hugh and Shirley Calf Robe and friends Charles Weasel Head and Irene Weasel Head died on the icy roads in a violent head-on collision with a semi-trailer just north of Fort Macleod. To add to the tragedy, one of the first vehicles on the scene was the bus carrying the Alberta boxing team back to Lethbridge.

A blizzard had hit during the fight card and worsened as the night had progressed. Right after the fight card the family headed home via Fort Macleod. I headed back at the same time, cutting across to Lethbridge right at Claresholm, on secondary Highway 520, joining up with Highway 23 near Barons. The snow was blowing down the highway, not across as on Highway 2, and wasn't creating too much of a problem. The others, on the overpass just before the Head Smashed-In turnoff along Highway 2, drove into swirling snow, blinding drivers in both lanes.

Members of the Alberta, British Columbia and Manitoba boxing teams were aboard a bus immediately behind the Calf Robe vehicle when the accident occurred and many members of the teams witnessed the accident, including Hugh Jr.

One of the first on the scene was Manitoba heavyweight Bill Turner. In a 1995 interview he said: "We left the bus to do what we could for those in the wreckage. Unfortunately one of the first to come upon the wreck was the Calf Robe boy. We restrained him and tried to console him the best we could, but you can just imagine what he was going through emotionally at seeing the accident. I sympathize with the Mills boy. He is Hugh Jr.'s best friend and he was quite shook up by the whole occurrence. I know I'm quite shaken and the rest of the boys on the bus were as well."

A number of the Alberta boxing team members were placed under sedation after the incident and Hugh Jr. was taken to the hospital suffering from severe shock. At one point the Alberta boxing team considered withdrawing from the competition, but the boys decided to continue in the tournament.

An air of depression clouded the Winter Games boxing at Claresholm the day after the deaths of Hugh Calf Robe Jr.'s parents. Alberta team members, particularly Alvin Mills of Cardston, a close friend of the young Calf Robe, seemed to go through motions during his bout on the card following the death of his friend's parents. In fact, all three Alberta boxers who fought on that card lost, including Mills.

The next night the boxing continued in Claresholm, under a pall of sadness. A minute's silence was held for the dead parents and friends of the young boxer and, as fate would have it, the first scheduled fight of the night featured Hugh Jr.'s friend Alvin Mills.

Alvin, who reportedly broke into tears as the bus passed the accident scene on the return trip to Claresholm the next day, was the first boxer to appear on the card. While he fought a good fight, one sensed the young boxer's heart was not in it and he dropped a unanimous decision to Mark Adams of New Brunswick in his 105-pound class.

"Adams kept driving into me," Alvin stated, "and I couldn't keep him off. I should have used my left jab a lot more. Adams is strong and he's in top shape."

The fists of Charlie Smallface were pretty potent as well, and earned him respect across Canada in the 1950s. He was an eight-time Alberta boxing champion, in divisions ranging from 70 to 139 pounds.

Back in 1958 there wasn't a boxer around who relished stepping into the ring with Charlie Smallface. The Kainai amateur fighter was one of the best this province has ever seen. He answered the bell 93 times during his amateur fistic career, and lost only four times.

The boxing ring is behind him, but Charlie finds new challenges on the golf course. And like his boxing, he is also ranked as one of this areas top shot-makers. In fact, he claims his most cherished moment in sport occurred on the golf course, not in the boxing ring.

"I've had a few memorable moments," said Charlie, who is now an avid horse race fan. "But one of

Garry Allison Photo

**The powerful fist of
Charlie Smallface**

65

the most memorable is a hole-in-one at Spokane in a golf tournament. It was on the 11th hole, a par three 200-yarder, and I used a four iron. The tee was way up high and the green down along the lake where it levelled off. It was my first hole-in-one."

"The first fight I lost is memorable," he pointed out with a laugh. "I had won 49 straight fights but I lost number 50 against Ronnie Paulsen in Edmonton. He went on that year to win the Canadian bantamweight championship. I figured I had won, but you can't argue with the judges. But Ronnie would never come down south for a rematch.

"Also, I remember a kid I fought from Peace River, Frank Belrose. We fought three times. The first one I won by a KO, but the last two were close, for provincial or Golden Gloves titles. I won them both. I also fought Eddie First Rider and Kai Yip in exhibition bouts." He fought in the Canadian finals twice, and was runner up both times. Charlie Smallface left the ring for good in 1959.

Perhaps the greatest boxer off the Kainai Nation was Eddie First Rider. The Toy Bulldog easily took the measure of Peter Schmidt June 28, 1963 with a unanimous decision in Lethbridge to win the Canadian professional welterweight championship.

Schmidt was no pushover. A year prior to meeting Eddie he had beaten the immortal Sugar Ray Robinson. But after his battle with Eddie, Schmidt stated he had never been up against a dirtier fighter. But, after all, it was pro boxing not a Japanese tea ceremony.

Promoter Bus Murdoch has many a tale about setting up this fight, and the follow up, in which Eddie was badly beaten on May 1, 1963 by a TKO in the sixth round. Eddie had a drinking problem, but if Bus could keep him out of reach of the booze he had a great fighter on his hands. He was unable to do that for the rematch.

Had Eddie won the return match he was scheduled to meet the then number one welterweight in the world, Casper "Indian" Ortega, a big-money match to be sure. But Eddie just couldn't deal with the training regime needed - if indeed he even tried - to remain at the top of his game.

Eddie First Rider was not only a good pro, he was a great amateur. Max Gibb fought on many amateur cards alongside Eddie. "He was tough even then and you could see he had the tools to be a great one," Max said of the now deceased First Rider. "Too bad he couldn't deal with it all."

Though not a member of the Kianai Nation, those with long hockey memories will remember Freddie Sasakamoose when he wheeled around the old Lethbridge Arena as a visiting player with the Moose Jaw Canucks in the early 1950s. By 1953 he was playing with the Chicago Blackhawks of the National Hockey League.

Born Christmas day, 1933 on the Whitefish (Big River) Reserve in Saskatchewan, Freddie started out on bobskates in 1938. In his hockey playing days he was noted for his dazzling speed and his accurate wrist shot. His career with Chicago was short lived, terminated by Freddie himself when he decided to return home to his reserve and the people he missed. "I just missed home," he told me one time at a Kianai Golf Tournament in Waterton.

A place I frequented on the Kainai Nation was the Kainai High School at Standoff. Seldom has a school done so much for the visibility and portrayal of Indian athletes as St. Mary's Kainai High School has since the early 1950s.

The Warrior and Warriorette teams carried the Kainai Nation's colours with honour, winning more than their share of championships. Despite its small size St. Mary's has won baseball, football and basketball titles on league to provincial levels. It spawned individual stars as well in cross-country and track and field events.

Warrior football began in 1960, preceded by the basketball program which met with almost immediate success.

Lethbridge Herald Photo
The Toy Bulldog, Eddie First Rider

Today, competing in the elite high school leagues, the Warriors and Warriorettes continue to shine.

There's a long list of top athletes that were St. Mary athletic standouts, including Jim Plume, Lionel Weasel Head - who starred for a number of years with Brandon in Canadian University basketball - Joe Scout, Marcel Weasel Head - now a Kainai Tribeal councillor - Lyle Standing Alone, Jordan and Mike Bruised Head, Gregg Eagle Plume, Danny Fox, Bill Mistaken Chief, Leroy Little Bear - prominent in university scholastic circles - Marvin Heavy Head and many, many others who have gone on to prominent roles on and off the reserve.

One of my prized possessions is a painting by former Warrior, Mark Brave Rock on behalf of the team. It hangs prominently in my family room.

Jim Plume has gone into horse racing, with some top-calibre horses, including two Quarter horse Futurity Cup winners and a Derby winner as well - all high-paying races. And speaking of horse racing, Calvin "Red" Chief Calf, who could drive the hoop with the best of them is a regular at Whoop-Up Downs.

Narcisse Blood, a standout in basketball for the Warriors and an outstanding quarterback in football, went on to win the Tom Longboat Award as the top Indian athlete in Canada. He also made his mark in political circles on the reserve and has served two terms on Council..

Two other outstanding athletes, both graduates of Kainai High School, Jocelyn Davis and Charlton Weasel Head received the Tom Longboat regional awards for outstanding achievements in athletics on the reserve and in Canada.

Davis, daughter of Jackie Davis and John Knife, was born in Cardston. She transferred to Tatsikiisaapo'p Middle School on the reserve and completed her education at Kainai High School. By Grade 9 she was a "floater" with the Kainai Lady Warriors basketball team and developed from being what she calls a "rangy post" to one of the top power forwards in southern Alberta. She received two regional Longboat awards during her career.

Charlton Weasel Head was a starting guard for the Brandon Bobcats, twice runners up for the Canadian university basketball championships. He played three years with the Lethbridge

The Longboat award is named in honour of Tom Longboat, one of the world's greatest distance runners and a member of the Six Nations in eastern Canada. This young Mohawk won the Boston Marathon in 1907 and finished second once.

He began running in 1905 and was one of the most consistent international distance runners of his time. Late in his career, during World War I, he served as a dispatch runner in France.

Community College Kodiaks and two with Brandon.

Weasel Head said through sports he learned to be proud of his native heritage, and to take part in that heritage. "You have to believe in yourself and not be afraid to dream," he said. "Once you put your mind to something there's no stopping you." Weasel Head is youngest child of Gloria Weasel Head and Norbert Fox.

Another Longboat winner from Alberta was Willie Littlechild. He won the Canadian Longboat award in 1967 and 1974. Willie, an Ermineskin Cree, won championships in hockey, swimming, basketball, triathlon, bull riding and golf. He became the first Alberta Indian to become a lawyer and the first elected to Parliament, as a Progressive Conservative, 1988-1993.

A top high school athlete was Gifford Fox, who starred in football with Cardston High School, despite chronic heart problems.

In recent times the Lady Warriors have been making a major impact on the southern Alberta basketball front. The former superintendent of schools for the reserve, Joyce Goodstriker, was a top athlete in her day and strongly believed in a quality sports program to compliment the academic programs of the reserve schools.

For many years it was the girls of the reserve who ignored sports and spent their time in school, going on to college and university. Today, the boys are joining them, excelling in athletics, but going on to college and university as well.

Jim Plume, born in 1960 at the Cardston Hospital, got bit by the bug in the late 1980s - the racing bug that is. "I got the bug when I went to Idaho with Godfrey Weasel Head and Mike Oka, and then when I had a winner, well there was no stopping me," Jim said with a big, satisfied laugh.

In 1998, it all came to an exciting pinnacle. Owner Jim - and his four silent partners - were all smiles Oct. 3, 1998 when Eye Scream captured the Canadian Quarter Horse Cup Futurity, flying over the 350-yard course in 17.88 seconds. The grey colt topped an elite field of eight two-year-olds in the $78,060 run, at that time the richest horse races in Canada for the speedy Quarter horses.

Despite leaving the sport for a while, Jim was still feeling the effects of the bug bite in 2007 and by 2008 he was partnered with old friend, Frank Weasel Head and the Chief of the Kainai Nation, Charlie Weasel Head, who'd had a contender in the 2007 Quarter Horse Derby. Like Jim, Charlie was back for another try at the big Futurity purse.

And low and behold, after 10 years Jim won the Futurity once again!

"Its incredible!" That's how Jim summed up his second win in the Canada Quarter Horse Cup Futurity Sept. 20, 2008 at the Rocky Mountain Turf Club. For the 12th running of the Futurity, he watched Tres D Man, trained by John Harris win the lion's share of the $102,500 race.

Chief Charlie, who had tried once before for a big win three years back and lost a close one in the Derby, was equally happy.

"This was worth the wait," he said. "When you get the seven top qualifiers likes this in a race, well anything can happen. This is great!"

In winning the 2008 Futurity, Jim and company shared the winner's purse of $44,444.

One year later in the 2009 Quarter Horse Canada Cup Derby - though only for a few

Billy Mills wins Gold in Tokyo

seconds in cool late afternoon on an October day - Jim, Chief Charlie and his wife Rhonda, were ecstatic. They had just watched Tres D Man do what no other horse in memory had ever done, win the Derby the year after it had won the Futurity.

But this isn't the only era where Kainai athletes have shown their skills. In 1926 Pat Weasel Head rode a bronc called Moonshine to a standstill to win the saddle bronc riding title at Cardston. The same year he won money at a rodeo near Cowley.

"In 1925, I won a saddle at Fort Macleod in the bronc riding too," Pat said in 1980, as he sat on the sidelines at a Standoff rodeo, remembering when he used to compete, from 1917 through the 1920s. "I won a rodeo on the reserve the same year, and won a bridle. I also won the Brocket stampede.

"The best Indian cowboy I ever saw was Pete Bruised Head Sr. He did everything, he roped, he rode, he did it all. I rodeoed for 14 years, but I only really made money in the 1920s," Pat commented.

Certainly a memorable moment for all Native people, and for anyone who follows the Olympic Games, came in 1964, when a young Lakota Sioux Billy Mills demonstrated what dedication to a goal can achieve. While not a southern Albertan, the story is one of inspiration for every young athlete.

"I can win! I can win!" Those were the thoughts running through a young Sioux boy's mind about 200 metres from the finish line at the Tokyo Olympics, despite the fact there were two runners ahead of him, including world champion Ron Clark. Seconds flashed by and Billy Mills was screaming in his mind, "I won! I won! I won!"

On that fateful day in 1964 in Tokyo, Mills became the Olympic 10,000-metre gold medalist, joining only a handful of North American Indians throughout history who have won Olympic gold.

"What a thrill, to know that for one day in your life you are the best in the world," said Mills during a visit to a Four-World seminar at the Lethbridge YWCA in the mid-1990s.

.Billy Mills had gone to the 18th Olympiad as an unknown - but a totally focussed unknown. In fact, he was so unknown a Japanese official grabbed him right after the gold-medal-winning run and asked, "Who are you? Who are you?"

Fact was he was a Lakota Sioux, a man with a goal, focused solidly on Olympic gold.

Halfway through the race Mills realized he was only one second off his fastest 5,000-metre race. He knew, at that pace, he couldn't finish the 10,000-metre run. He wanted to quit. But he didn't. With only 200 metres left, and passed by Clark and a Kenyan runner, he wanted to quit again. But he didn't.

"People who are focussed on positive desires never quit, they are focussed to succeed," said Mills.

The last time an American had won a medal in the Olympic 10,000 metres had been 1912. Then along came this Lakota Sioux, a so-so competitor from the University of Kansas.

"When I went to those Games I was so focussed nothing disturbed me," said Mills, whose wife Patricia was in the stands for his history-making run.

Mills' training was intensely focused; for more than a four-year period prior to the Olympics he would run 100 miles a week. He followed the childhood advice of his father - find a positive desire in your life, know yourself and succeed.

"Only when you are self-motivated will you succeed," Mills said, adding that all people, young and old, should start being around others with positive desires.

Billy spoke of his

Lakota Sioux runner Billy Mills

running days, when his buddies would try to entice him to party with them. When he declined they'd even beat him up because he didn't go. One time he did go, and his buddies fed him a doctored drink and left him in freezing weather to sleep it off, outside behind a building.

His uncle found him and literally saved him from freezing to death.

He also spoke of a time he refused to go with a carload of his friends to a pow-wow, and took the bus instead. He later learned that group of buddies had died in a car crash while on their way.

From those days, to the thrill of the Olympic Games to serving as a 2nd Lieutenant in the U.S. Marine Corps, to marriage and raising three daughters and three other adopted daughters, Billy Mills has become a symbol of success for all peoples.

Two years prior to the 1964 Olympics Billy Mills made a commitment to himself about Olympic gold.

Billy Mills - subject of the 1984 Hollywood movie Running Brave, starring Robbie Benson and featuring Rufus Goodstriker of the Kainai Nation - went to Tokyo having previously only run four 10,000-metre races. No one even thought of him, not with Clark, the favoured Australian, in the field.

With graduation from high school Mills had 18 scholarship offers, and he chose the U of K. His experiences at Kansas were shocking. He wasn't allowed to join a fraternity or room with his white or Black friends because he was an Indian.

"I was not prepared for the rejection I would be given by the dominant society in America," said Mills, who was raised on the Pine Ridge Reservation in South Dakota. "It hurt."

After his success in Tokyo, Mills became a self-made success, director of Billy Mills Enterprises and a past

> *Ironically, years later in the foreign land of Japan, Billy Mills felt at home.*
>
> *"For the first time in my life I was in a country where the colour of the people's skin was my colour. I felt extremely comfortable and I was at home there."*

member of President Clinton's Fitness and Sports Council. He accepts numerous speaking engagements each year from marketing and sales groups to native organizations and workshops.

Ken Tailfeathers Sr. witnessed many changes on the Kainai Nation during the last 30 years of his life, as well as in rodeo and horse racing, sports he excelled at, and pioneered. It was a case of the old days being the best days for a late respected Kainai Elder.

"It was a risky road back in the 1940s and 1950s, but a happy life, that's about all you got out of rodeo because you spent all you made," Ken said shortly before his death in August of 1988.

Ken remembered his younger days on the reserve when as kids they used to entice two bulls into the same pasture and watch them fight. He recalled the days when cars and trucks were a secondary mode of transportation. Horses used to be led or driven to rodeos at Pincher Creek, Fort Macleod and Lethbridge back in the early 1930s, he said.

Ken was a tough, capable calf roper. He was second in the Canadian standings twice and second at the Calgary Stampede in 1952. He also served as a pickup man at Calgary for 21 years, a job he loved.

"I rodeoed for 45 summers - that's quite a while," Ken said. "I roped calves from 1936 until 1965. We used to have a lot of fun at rodeos then, with fiddle music and dancing. We were a close group. I never had any problems - when I was asked by a bartender back then if I was Indian, I'd laugh and tell him, 'no, I'm smoked Irish.'

"When Fred Gladstone and I started roping we used to practise on the open prairie - badger and gopher holes didn't make any difference. We had fun. Fred and I and a bunch of others started the IRCA too." Of all the Indian cowboys during the years, Ken said Frank Many Fingers and Jimmy Wells Sr. were two of the best.

In 1976 Ken Tailfeathers switched interests, turning to horse racing. His first horse, Barbie's Finale, hooked him on the sport, he said. Among his favourites, and best, were a Quarter horse, Bar Azure and a Thoroughbred, My Son Warren. Both were also favourites with bettors at Whoop-Up Downs in Lethbridge. Bar Azure won Horse of the Year honours for the B circuit in the mid-1980s, said Ken's son Ira Tailfeathers.

"We were really proud of him when the horse received that saddle and blanket at High River," said Ira. "Dad was a real good horseman. Bar Azure had run at Raymond in 1979 just after my brother Punch's daughter Charmaine died. Punch asked me to ride and win for her; but I was a little too big. We really wanted to win the race for her so I asked Elijah Bourne to ride for us, and that told the story. He won."

Ira trained many of his Dad's top horses, including Bar Azure, Miss Stormy Reed, Peral's Choice, Grassy's Last Gas, Miss Barbie's Finale, My Son Warren, Slow Hand Man, Alert Bay and Tesky Road.

Grassy's Last Gas was a good horse which Ken bought from Jim Munro, who says he won the first race at Trout Springs.

"We had to re-break him though," Ira said with a laugh. "Grassy was kind of special to me. He was a one-man horse and I was the man. For me he was real special. I raced him once two weeks in a row, over three furlongs and he won both. After that we put him in five furlong races. He won five or six straight races at Whoop-Up Downs in the 1980s."

Ken Tailfeathers died August 21, 1988 at age 71 while at a race meet in Kalispell, Montana, right in the winner's circle. He had just won a race with Grassy's Last Gas. Ira still has the winner's circle picture with the horse and his Dad, taken just minutes before Ken collapsed.

"On the same day, My Son Warren was up in Lethbridge and he won that day as well," said Geoff Healy.

This made Ken's last two races winning ones. It was a great way to go out; he would have liked it that way said Ira.

Ken would keep his horses at home, just east of St. Paul's school, in the Bullhorn area of the reserve. He'd gallop them in the field at first, but he later had a small track on his place. However, Ira said his Dad preferred to see the horse gallop in the field rather than on the small track.

My Son Warren won the Labatts Marathon Series in Grande Prairie that year and was named Horse of the Year in Lethbridge. As well, Ken was named owner of the year in Lethbridge. My Son Warren also set the track record in Lethbridge in 1985 when he won the Georgina Williams Memorial Stake, along with the winner's share of the purse of $3,470. Doug Hall was in the irons for the mile and an eighth run.

"You know, Grandpa (Ken) always used to say, never fall in love with a horse," said Geoff Healy. "But when Rod Haynes claimed My Son Warren one time, Grandpa claimed him right back the next race. He loved that horse."

Geoff was one of 28 grandchildren at the time of Ken's death. Geoff's father Dave, was a top trainer in his own right and had won Derbies in Medicine Hat and High River in 1976, with Stormies First Light. The same time Dave and others used regular pony horses as runners just to keep Quarter horse racing alive at some of the smaller tracks in southern Alberta.

"My dad and men like Charlie Ivins, Jerry Going, Garnet Leech, Jim Chipman, Jim Munro and others . . . they're the ones who kept Quarter horse racing alive when things were dying out in the 1970s," said Geoff. "My dad was also one of the first natives to train horses for other people, like Jerry Stogan of Sexsmith and later for Chuck Stogan."

Ken and wife Helen (Quesnelle), whom he married in 1936, had five sons, Tuffy, Butch, Leslie (Punch), Ira and Keith (Punky), and four daughters, Caroline, Shirley, Beverly and Byrdeen.

Ken was born on the Kainai Nation and attended St. Paul's Residential School. Leaving school he farmed and ranched and then worked for the CPR, and for 20 years was employed by the Blood Band. He was one of the founders of the Kainai Nation School Bus Co-Op. His sporting interests included the Kainai Resrerve Boxing Club and support of Minor Hockey in Cardston.

This runner-up for the Canadian calf roping championship in 1931 had a love of horse racing dating back to the 1930s, when he began match-racing his horses. In 1976 Ken began racing with the Canada West Racing Association and into Montana as well.

Those who knew Ken Tailfeathers remember him as a gentleman and a kind, loving father whose influence led his boys into rodeo and horse racing as well.

Its hard to top a world championship, be it in the Olympics or in the sport of rodeo. Even in a career where he recorded three Canadian championships, record runs and record earnings, a world title has to dominate the thinking of the Kainai's premiere calf roper, Jim Gladstone.

Jim Gladstone, whose face has adorned posters and the programs for the Canadian Finals Rodeo, almost made it two world titles in a row. However, a broken rope on his last calf cost Gladstone a very definite shot at his second consecutive world calf roping championship in Oklahoma City in December of 1978.

"My most memorable moment has to be the winning of the world calf roping championship in 1977," Jimmy stated. "When Paul Tierney missed his calf and I knew that I had won - I just couldn't believe it. That championship was the big thing for me, it was something I had dreamed about all my life.

"I guess you could say the saddest moment in the rodeo arena was the broken rope," he added with a laugh. Had Gladstone's rope not broken on his last calf at the 1978 world championships he would likely have won the final go round and earned enough in the overall average to make it title number two.

"I've also had some memorable moments in basketball. The only time I ever coached we won the city championships in Calgary with the Crescent Heights JV team. We lost our first seven games that year, but won everything from that point on. Also playing on Doug's (Clark's seniors) basketball team when we beat Port Alberni and Winnipeg was a big thrill."

Really, Jimmy's achievements are almost uncountable in his sport. Along with the fact he returned to school as an adult and went on to become a lawyer. He was the leading calf roper in Canada five times going into the Canadian Finals; he is three-time Canadian calf roping champion; and has won the Canadian Indian Rodeo Cowboys Association calf roping title. He was "flagged out" which cost him the Calgary Stampede roping championship when his calf kicked

Herald Photo
Calf roper Jim Gladstone

71

loose. He had been a Christmas Tournament all-star in basketball and appeared on national television on Front Page Challenge and the former CBC late night talk show.

Jimmy's outstanding moments have been numerous, but the highlight will always be from 1977 when he became the first Canadian and first Blackfoot Indian to ever win a world championship in a rodeo timed event, the world calf roping championship.

Jim had some big boots to fill as he followed his father Fred into rodeo. But then Fred Gladstone had set the pace for many Indian rodeo competitors in Canada.

In 1948 Fred Gladstone became the first Indian cowboy to win a Canadian calf roping championship and to prove it was no accident he followed it up with a championship in 1950. He worked for the Calgary Stampede, spending two decades officiating infield events. Fred was also one of the founding members of the Indian Rodeo Cowboy Association in 1967 and worked for many years as a timed event judge at the Calgary Stampede.

And up until Father Time finally caught up with Fred he was active in oldtimer rodeo events. He passed away in 2009.

Fred, one of the most personable of all cowboys, with his ever-present smile, was one of the people who made it easier for the Indian competitor on the professional rodeo circuit.

The Indian Rodeo Cowboys Associatiion

I remember Fred Gladstone making me laugh one day, with a sad reality. After listening to one of the oldtime white cowboys lamenting about how tough they had it in the "old days" in the smaller towns, where no one wanted cowboys in the hotels or restaurants. Fred quietly pointed out: "You think that was rough . . . what about us Indian cowboys?"

Gladstone Family Photo
Fred Gladstone, with a calf on

spawned such great cowboys as Pete Bruised Head, the always tough Levi Blackwater; Kelvin Fox has won three World All-Indian bareback titles; and Hank Bruised Head with a bull riding crown under his belt. Bill T. Head and Lewis Little Bear are all past World All-Indian saddle bronc champions as well, and Stan Wells earned a steer wrestling title.

Levi Blackwater, was a good friend, and enjoyed his finest year in rodeo in 1972, after 15 years in the business. Besides winning money on the Chinook and Foothills amateur circuits, Levi cleaned up on the All-Indian circuit, winning the steer wrestling title and placing second in the all around standings. He also finished in the top 10 in the calf roping.

Levi was always telling me about the finer points of the game, but he never did convince me to climb on a horse and give bull dogging a try. I had no plans of leaving a horse racing at 35 mph.

Born in Cardston in 1936, Levi made his home on the Kainai Nation. His first taste of rodeo action came at a southern Alberta Roping Club meet in 1957 and since that time his name used to pop up everywhere, from the Calgary Stampede to shows at Brooks, Lethbridge, Raymond, Vulcan and Foremost.

A quiet, almost shy man, Levi was a member of the Canadian Rodeo Cowboys Association but later competed only at the Chinook amateur rodeos and on the IRCA circuit. His main events were steer wrestling and calf roping but he also entered team roping and bull riding - as a younger man.

I remember Levi's skills and grit best from a pro rodeo in Vulcan. We stood in the penalty box of the arena before the rodeo, chatting about things in general and his sore shoulder in particular. He had hurt it rodeoing and it was all he could do to lift his arm shoulder high without wincing in pain. Despite that he had no intention of turning out. Levi took his steer, sore shoulder and all. He did it so well in fact that he won the rodeo, beating many past and future Canadian and world champions in the process - with only one good arm.

I know of very few others, Pete Bruised Head for one, who had abilities equal to Levi, who competed despite the pains and who were among the strongest men I've ever met.

With Levi's death in April of 1991, rodeo on the Kainai Nation, and rodeo in general, lost a true friend. But even more devastating, was the fact I and many, many others, lost a personal friend. I still miss his quiet, unassuming ways, his dry humour and being haled with "hello my friend" every time he saw me.

I was both honoured and saddened when I spoke at Levi's funeral in the jam-packed indoor rodeo arena at Standoff. Earlier I had been honoured by the family when I was asked to speak at Levi's daughter Jackie's marriage (to Lewis Little Bear) at the Lodge in Lethbridge.

Levi's been gone many years now - he died from a fall from the bleachers at a rodeo in the Standoff Agriplex. A few days later those same bleachers were packed to capacity for his funeral.

People in the know still talk about Levi Blackwater and his prowess in the rodeo arena. Injuries were a source of trouble throughout his career. He suffered two broken legs, two broken collar bones and was constantly handicapped in competition by recurring knee trouble. However, he overcame those injuries by luck - luck of the draw that is. It is almost uncountable the number of times Levi had the final steer or final calf at a rodeo, no matter on which circuit, and that is a great advantage.

"You know just what you have to do, so you can just go all out on that final run and do it," he once said. Despite his age, 55 at his death, he was still throwing a rope with the best of them, and was organizing weekend jackpot rodeos at Standoff.

Danger and death seem to be present in any sport, but perhaps moreso in rodeo. On July 17, 1961 tragedy hit the world famous Calgary Stampede when Willie Little Bear, a 25-year-old

Garry Allison Photo

**Levi Blackwater
a multi-event rodeo star**

Kainai Nation saddle bronc rider was killed in the afternoon in the rodeo arena, trampled to death by a bronc. Little Bear had drawn a horse named Grizzly Sal, a 10-year-old, 545-kilogram bronc owned by the Bruce family of Calgary. The bronc had stood quietly in the chutes and for the first few jumps Willie was in control, but he caught his foot in the stirrup as he was bucked off and swung down under the big grey bronc. He was kicked in the head, resulting in multiple skull fractures. It was the first and only time a person has been killed during the infield events at Calgary, dating back to 1912.

Willie died at the Holy Cross Hospital in Calgary at 10:10 p.m., about eight hours after the accident. His wife Agnes and two of his brothers witnessed the accident. Besides Agnes he left three children behind. Willie was buried back on the Kainai Nation in the cemetery along the St. Mary's School road, off nearby Highway 2. The Calgary Stampede paid all his funeral expenses.

Certainly every cowboy knows he lives with the threat of death and more likely injury every time he enters the rodeo arena. To this day I always tell Pete Bruised Head, a Kainai rodeo legend for more than 40 years, that it's a wonder he doesn't rattle when he walks. That's how often he'd broken most of the bones in his body.

Upon hearing the list of broken bones Peter suffered in rodeo, it's amazing those bones don't clang around inside his six-foot-1.5-inch, 195 pound frame.

"I think I might have three or four bones that haven't been broken," he said with a laugh. Pete spent virtually all of 1970 and 1971 on crutches, but it didn't stop him from riding - I sat with him once as he cut a cast off his leg in order to climb on his bull. When the ride ended, friends helped him out of the arena and took him to the hospital to have a new cast put on his broken leg.

"I've broken my jaw, nose, both arms, both wrists, both legs - one of them five times, punctured a lung, smashed all the ribs on my right side, broken one or more ribs 19 times, been kicked in the head twice and broken my tail bone.

"Most of those injuries happened in the chute. That's where the real danger was. Getting out of the chute in one piece was always a problem. Rodeo was a sport I loved. I made a little money at it, but I did it because I enjoyed it. It was the competition, the sport itself. Once it got into your blood it stayed there. It was hard to quit."

It is ironic that one of his worst riding accidents came at home while he was working on his place. He'd been working with his cattle and while climbing a cutbank it gave way. Had he not been able to somehow get back on his horse and slowly plod for home he would likely have died in the field.

In today's age, where cowboys tend to specialize in one, and at best, two events, Pete was a true all around cowboy. He was also a former Alberta Golden Gloves light heavyweight boxing champion, in 1960.

Pete won prize money in every rodeo event conceivable except the ladies barrel race. Besides the three major riding events, and the two timed ones, he has ridden as an outrider in chuckwagon racing, decorated steers, joined the wild horse race, the wild cow milking and team roping. His favourite event, though he claimed it was not his best, was saddle bronc riding.

Later in life he said with a laugh: "I guess team roping is my best event.

"The hardest was steer decorating. It was worse than bull riding. You just had to slap the ribbon on and then prepare yourself for a wreck almost every time."

Pete, born in Cardston in 1936, rodeoed hard for about a quarter of a century. He climbed a long way up the ladder from his first rodeo at Raymond, in the amateur saddle bronc riding. In fact, he'd have trouble getting all his various awards in one room.

Garry Allison Photo
The personable Pete Bruised Head in 1979

"I won somewhere around 30 saddles I guess, over 100 buckles and around 30 or 35 trophies. At a California rodeo in 1969 I won a two-year-old registered Quarter horse stallion, with a saddle, four buckles and a pair of boots. I won a lot of money too, but it went for gasoline, cattle, food, motels, entry fees and living in general."

Another item he could have added was the amount he paid out each year joining various associations. He belonged to the Canadian Rodeo Cowboys Association, the Indian Rodeo Cowboy Association, the Northern IRCA, the American IRCA, and the Rodeo Cowboys Association in the United States. He left his mark in every association he joined.

Always competitive on the CRCA and RCA, circuits, Pete dominated the all-Indian circuits to which he belonged. The huge all-Indian rodeos in Arizona and New Mexico proved fairly lucrative for Pete over the years. The number of entries at these rodeos was staggering. More than 300 bull riders and doggers were not uncommon and often the bareback riders and calf ropers numbered near the 250 mark.

"They have an awful lot of Indians down there to draw from," Pete said. "There were over 60,000 Navajos and Apaches in the same area."

One of the best weekends he ever had in the rodeo arena came at the Western State Indian Rodeo Association Finals in Omak, Washington. He won the bareback bronc riding and the all around title, finished second in the saddle bronc event, and placed in the steer wrestling, calf roping and team roping, taking home about $3,000. And that was in the mid 1970s when Canadian year-long titles were won with less.

Pete won the Indian Rodeo Cowboys Association all around title in 1967 and 1974, the saddle bronc title in 1967 and 1973, and bareback title in 1967, 1973 and 1974.

Rodeo was a full time job for Pete, a father of seven. He and his wife Margaret - a truly wonderful woman who passed away a few years back - had two girls, Henny Marie and Tina and five boys, Wright, Allan, Lynn, Clinton and Ivan. Pete and Margaret raised another three boys, Les, Larry and Casey Scott, after their parents, Margaret's brother and wife, were killed in a car accident.

You will go a long way before you find a wife and mother like Margaret. As far a I'm concerned, she was Number One.

Contracts, where rodeo committees paid to have a specific contestant attend their rodeo, were normal in some of the circuits where Pete rodeoed. In fact he found himself on the receiving end of these benefits from time to time.

Travelling around the country, 35 to 40,000 miles a year, pulling a horse trailer containing two horses, was not an easy life.

"Everything seemed to go up sky high when I came to town," he said. "Hotels, food, clothes all seemed to cost more. I very seldom ran into that in later years though, but in the late '50s and '60s there was a lot of that for rodeo people, but especially we Indian rodeo cowboys."

Pete Jr, came by his skills honestly. Pete Bruised Head Sr. was the Calgary Stampede calf roping champion in 1925 and 1927. He was also a top bronc rider, competing against some of the best of the 1920s, such as the legendary Pete Knight.

He liked to practice and was well prepared physically for the demanding sport of rodeo, as was Pete Jr., who was as solid as a fireplug.

Pete Jr. was a big, burly man, strong as an ox, and few people dared mess with him. He served as the only policeman on the Kainai Nation for quite a spell, without a gun.

When I asked him about that, he just laughed, made a huge fist, and said "this will stop 'em as quick as a bullet."

After all the years about the only thing that changed in rodeo for Pete was "the ground seemed a lot harder as I grew older."

**Bobby Gottfriedson
a top saddle bronc rider**

Some pretty fair Indian rodeo competitors have come out of these big rodeos, including Pete, Bud Connelly, Larry Condon and Bobby Gottfriedson.

I sat with Bobby Gottfriedson one time at the Canadian Finals and he told me about the first time he entered the Calgary Stampede, and ran into one of the judges coming out of the office.

"The guy asked me if I'd entered, and I told him I had. He looked me in the eye and said 'As long as I'm a judge here no Indian will ever win.'"

Well, that idiot quit judging a few years later and Bobby won the bronc riding at Calgary. That's what Indian cowboys ran into time and time again.

Stan Wells doesn't beat around the bush about rodeo, he comes right out and lays it on the line: "Rodeo is my life," the 2000 Indian National Finals Rodeo steer wrestling champion said. "When you win, you can make a good living at it, but when you don't, it can be pretty tough."

The Kainai bulldogger was 29 when he won a championship saddle and silver buckle in Albuquerque, New Mexico at the huge INFR get together, featuring the top Indian cowboys from throughout North America.

He came home with the hardware, and more than $3,000 US, for 19.6 seconds total work in the arena on four steers.

"It was the first time I qualified for the INFR, and it was sure worthwhile," he said with a laugh. My main priority had been the pro rodeos these past few years, but with injuries I've had a rough couple of years, until the Albuquerque Finals."

Stan, whose father Robert Wells was a bull rider and steer wrestler in his younger days, grew up around the rodeo arena. It became a way of life for him. His first rodeo was right at home during Kainai Indian Days at Standoff, as a kid in the steer riding. He went on to try some of the riding events as he grew older, but found his real interest was bull dogging.

"I didn't do too well that first rodeo, I was more into hockey back then. I played junior hockey on the reserve, with the Kainai Golden Chiefs and then went on to the Senior A Braves.

"In rodeo, bull dogging looked like it would be real fun, and you can last a lot longer at it. Right off the start my Dad showed me some stuff and then I went to some bull dogging schools, with Bob Wilson and Andrew Hunt. I roped a bit when I was younger, and now I'm getting back into it, calves and team roping."

Stan bull dogged off a team of horses owned by his hazer, Dean Louis of Hobbema. "It was about 1997 when I owned my last horses, so I used Dean's."

Stan's first win at a big rodeo came in 1992, in Shelby, Montana. He has carried his pro card since 1995 and rodeos hard on the pro circuit - when he's healthy. A broken collar bone, playing hockey December of 1999, kept him out of rodeo much of the 2000 year, healing up just in time to catch top IRCA events and qualify for the INFR out of the Northern Alberta Native Cowboys Association.

Stan Wells left Kainai High School early, but was picking up courses along the way. He completed an interior finishing course, specializing in flooring, at Mount Royal College in Calgary. Along with Wells at the 2000 INFR was a veteran Kainai cowboy, going back to the Finals in what most would consider rocking chair age.

In the sport of bareback bronc riding, 30 is old age. Kelvin Fox scoffed at such a thought. At Albuquerque Fox was riding bareback broncs at the New Mexico show, and not only was he climbing on the high-kicking, dirty ducking broncs at age 45 he was doing it in championship style. Despite the fact this father of six, and a grandfather as well, was considered too old to rodeo, he won his third championship buckle at the world's all-Indian finals, in grand fashion.

Fox put together rides of 77, 78, 68 and 72, to win

Garry Allison Photo
Kelvin Fox rodeoed even as a grandfather

two second place finishes in the go-rounds and the average in the four go-rounds at the INFR. He picked up more than $3,500 in cash, a trophy saddle and another silver buckle.

"Guys told me I didn't look like 45, and I tell them its all in your head, it's just a number. I get a kick out of the young kids, generations younger than me, when they tell me I might be 45 when I get on, but I'm 18 when the gate opens. I just loved getting in those broncs, just like Ty Murray said in that Wrangler ad. That's why I stayed with it so long. But you do age, you do slow down. Your mind said you can still do it, but sometimes your body is telling you another thing."

Going into the INFR people were telling him it would be a miracle if he won it all. After all, he'd won his first championship buckle at the very first INFR in 1976, in the bull riding at Salt Lake City. And it was way back in 1984 when he won buckle number two, this time in the bareback event, at Albuquerque.

Kelvin, who lives on the southeast end of the Kainai Nation, on land overlooking the house once lived in by famous Kainai cowboy Tom Three Persons, grew up around livestock and started his rodeo career with a win, at the Greatest Outdoor Show On Earth.

It was 1968 his Uncle Grant Fox interrupted Kelvin when he was practicing for a track and field meet, and gave him an entry form for the Calgary Stampede's boys' steer riding. He filled it out, got on some practice steers at the family ranch near the Gladstone Hall, and went to Calgary and won it all.

"I got hooked then and there, and I thought I'd never see a poor day again in my life," Kelvin said with a laugh. From there he moved through high school rodeo, winning the Alberta steer wrestling title, and on into the Chinook rodeo, the Indian Rodeo Cowboys Association and the pro ranks.

In 1996 and 1999 he won the Chinook Association's bareback titles and he's won the IRCA title seven times. On the pro circuit he never quite made it to the CFR, but he did win the Edmonton Super Rodeo, has placed at Rodeo Royal in Calgary, the Cheyenne Frontier Days, Whoop-Up Days in Lethbridge and many other top rodeos. "Looking back, I regret not sticking with it, but its too late now," he said.

In 2000 Kelvin made money at a lot of the big southwestern United States Indian rodeos, and won, or placed, at IRCA rodeos at Standoff, Brocket, Gleichen, Morley and the Tsuu T'ina. He knew he had a real shot at the Finals, if everything went well. He also knew it was going to be his last shot.

"That was the end of the riding, I've got nothing to prove. I got out while I was on top. The 2000 championship this year was the icing on the cake for me."

Those who knew Kelvin Fox throughout his rodeo career, knew he was destined to be one of the greats of the sport. In Indian rodeo circles he became a legend, winning world Indian titles 25 years apart, in a sport where 10 years is a great career.

Along the way Kelvin bounced back from adversity, from injuries in the rodeo arena - "I've never had to stay in hospital long because of injuries though". However self-inflicted problems have impacted his career..

"I had a weakness for alcohol," he said matter of factly. "I felt like I could have made the NFR and the CFR. I rode with a lot of world champions and I competed well with them, but I spent a lot of time partying and not taking care of business. But I've rodeoed so long now, it's too late to make up the years I lost. I could really kick myself in the butt. I see these young kids today, partying and riding and it bothers me."

Fox got into rodeo through his uncle, Grant Fox, who taught him to ride steers. In 1979 Kelvin went to his first rodeo school - three years after he'd won an INFR buckle - with world bareback champion Bruce Ford. He hadn't been on a bull since 1980, when a severe groin tear moved him out of that event. Since then, this cowboy who remembered going out to the barn daily in 30-below weather as a kid with his Dad, Richard Sr., and Uncle Grant to feed the horses, stuck to the bareback broncs, in every sense of the word.

Kelvin was around so long he was actually rodeoing, not only against the children of his former colleagues but one or two grandchildren and grand-nephews as well. He said the key to his longevity was constantly working out and keeping his 150-pound, 5-foot-10 frame in shape.

Fox completed his school at Cardston High School and spent about three years at Brigham Young University, studying agricultural economics and physical education. But rodeo and partying got in the way of school.

In 2000 he and wife Claudine lived on the reserve and Kelvin owned and operated his own school bus for the Blood School Bus Co-Op. The driver's seat is far more comfortable than a bronc.

He said the best bronc he'd ever been on had to be Calgary's Lonesome Me, a former bareback and saddle bronc of the year.

"You know, I never did draw Reg Kesler's Moonshine or Three Bars, but Uncle Grant was on Three Bars. There's a picture he said is his claim to fame, Three Bars up in the air kicking and Grant on the ground under her. In the states, they say the Kesler horses are probably the rankest of any going down the road. But Lonesome Me was probably my best, and some of the Kesler horses were the worst buckers. There's always some horse you just don't like getting on, and some good ones you do."

Kelvin sort of patterned his spurring style after Bruce Ford, a former world champion who also taught Marvin Garret to ride, and he liked the way champion Joe Alexander rode. Kelvin always admired the great Kainai cowboys like Pete Bruised Head, the macho man of the sport, and men like Fred and Jimmy Gladstone. His Uncle Grant Fox is also high on his list.

"When I first saw Lewis (Little Bear, the friend who had encouraged Kelvin to rodeo one more year) ride at Jim Gladstone's old arena, he was a natural and he just tapped off with his very first bronc. Some just have it. He won the INFR saddle bronc championship once. I was also proud of Stan Wells. It was nice to see him win the steer wrestling championship at the INFR the same year I won my last championship."

Rodeo judging, especially if you're an Indian bronc rider competing outside the Indian Rodeo Cowboys Association, is always questionable, but Kelvin said he kind of learned to roll with the flow.

"I've been gifted and I've been screwed. But

no matter what you did or said, they were not going to change their mind."

Kelvin is concerned about the future of rodeo on the reserve. The young people seem to be shunning the western mode of dress, opting for baggy pants and ear rings, like all youth. As well, there's less of a desire to go into sports of any type.

In Kelvin Fox's words, "Kids are too tied up with computers and Nintendo, the interest in rodeo just doesn't seem to be there. None of the kids today are as active as we used to be, it sure is a different age. When I was a kid, I'd go outside in the morning and we'd play outside all day. I worry about the future of my sport."

Of all the people I had to research on a second-hand basis - meaning they were long dead when I wrote about them - Tom Three Persons is one man I truly wish I had known first hand.

Born in 1886, a year before the signing of Treaty 7, Tom Three Persons was 26 when he went to Calgary the first-time. The six-foot-two, handsome, lithe athlete, left there a hero not only of his Kainai people, but of the entire rodeo world.

Tom was deeply involved in two of my favourite sports, horse racing and saddle bronc riding. As well he was a Kainai who moved among the whites with ease, in an era when things like that were uncommon, to say the least.

Tom lived in an era not too far removed from the settling of the west, and at the same time walked with men like Guy Weadick, Patrick Burns and others who were holding on to the past, yet at the same time striving to build a future.

For an in depth look at Three Persons read Hugh Dempsey's book: *Tom Three Persons - Legend of an Indian Cowboy.* But here's what I've been able to put together from other sources and interviews with some of his acquaintances.

It was the big high-heeled cowboy boots and the way Tom Three Persons carried himself that the late Lyman Turner of Magrath remembered best. Three Persons would regularly visit the

Tom Three Persons, champion bronc rider and race horse trainer

Magrath Trading Company store, where Turner was hardware manager. This was years after the tall, straight-backed Kainai bronc rider had made his mark at the famous Calgary Stampede.

"He was very striking to look at," Lyman said. "Tom used to come into Magrath a lot back in the 1940s."

In 1912 Three Persons was just one of many Native bronc riders, calf ropers and steer riders from the Kainai, Stoney, Piikani, Tsuu Tina and Siksika Nations invited to take part in the first Calgary Stampede. It is an unsubstantiated thought that the move was more of an advertising ploy than an idea any of these top Indian rodeo stars would actually win.

But Tom Three Persons grew up riding wild broncs. He went to Calgary a virtual unknown - known only to family and friends as a good bronc rider. He left the Stampede as world saddle bronc champion and established himself as a name that would live forever in rodeo history. He had done reasonably well on his first broncs at the Stampede, but on the final day he drew the great bronc Cyclone, owned by the Blanccett family. Cyclone ranked right up there with Midnight and Steamboat as the best of the best.

Cyclone was said to be unridable and had left about 130 top bronc riders sitting in the arena dust attesting to the fact he was one rank bronc.

The big black bronc's favourite move was to rear wildly, balancing on his hind legs, seemingly about to topple over, and then return to the earth with a bone-jarring thud as the front legs hit the ground. He would sun fish, dip and dive, shedding riders as he went. Until he met up with Tom Three Persons.

In 1912 the rodeo broncs were snubbed and held as the cowboy climbed on in mid-arena. They were not saddled and mounted in bucking chutes as they are today, which made for a much tougher start. Three Persons checked the cinch, pulling it tight, swung his long legs over the bronc's back, secured his high-crowned cowboy hat and said "let him go!"

A ride wasn't eight or 10 seconds back then; it lasted until the cowboy was bucked off or the bronc quit bucking.

On that September afternoon Tom took everything Cyclone had to offer and rode the great bronc to a stand-still.

Guy Weadick was quoted in the Canadian Cattleman magazine years later as saying Three Persons "hit him (Cyclone) in both shoulders with his spurs - and hard." Cyclone wasn't used to such treatment.

He reared high and went into his usual pattern of bucking. But Tom kept applying the steel. Cyclone got mad and really started in to buck and did everything on his list to try and unseat the rider who kept hitting him with his spurs at every jump.

"The horse finally quit bucking and stood still," Weadick was quoted as saying about the great ride. The ride was over. The crowd erupted. A new world champion saddle bronc rider, and a new hero, was crowned. Along with the standing ovation and adulation that lasted the remainder of his life, Tom Three Persons received one thousand dollars, a medal, a hand-made trophy saddle, a championship belt and a gold and silver mounted buckle. Tom was always partial to wearing almost knee-high cowboy boots with high heels with his pants tucked into the tops of the boots. He also liked to wear bright neck scarves and when riding donned red angora chaps. He was a striking figure.

After taming the great Cyclone to win the world saddle bronc championship at Calgary, Three Persons continued to compete in rodeo and won almost every rodeo he attended during his prime. He was making good money in the sport, as well as in horse racing, and had invested wisely in cattle and made a profit at horse trading.

Lyman said the wild grass on Three Persons' home ranch, just below the St. Mary's Dam spillway today and a few kilometres west of Spring Coulee, was ideal for the large cattle herds he raised. The corrals were the best quality, the house was large for its time and the barn was ideal for his ranching needs.

Rodeo and ranching were dangerous occupations though and Tom was always being treated for broken arms, ribs and other assorted aches and pains.

He returned to the Calgary Stampede again in 1923 - Weadick did produce another "greatest show on earth" in 1919 however - but Tom never did match the success he attained at his first Stampede. Father Time had taken his toll.

Despite the injuries he was one of the most successful raisers of Thoroughbred horses and purebred Herefords in southern Alberta. His horses ran almost yearly at the Raymond Stampede and Race Meet, winning their share of purses. As well, Tom and his horses appeared at almost every southern Alberta Fair and race day.

In 1946 Three Persons suffered a serious horse-oriented accident from a which he never recovered, leading eventually to his death in 1949 at age 63.

"There was a horse stampede on his ranch and the horses knocked down a gate on top of him," Lyman Turner said. "Many of the horses jumped or galloped across that gate and when they were finished Tom was broke up pretty bad. That was the beginning of the end for Tom as far as his health was concerned."

The rodeo champion never really recovered from the broken pelvis and other injuries. Most of his final years he carried a poplar staff to serve as a walking cane.

In the summer of 1949 Tom took ill and Blood Indian Agent Ralph Ragan took him to a hospital in Calgary. A month later Tom was dead.

At the time of his death in 1949 his cattle holdings alone were worth $80,000. Hundreds of people, white and Indian, attended his funeral at St. Mary's Catholic Church in Cardston, laying one of rodeo's great legends to rest.

The shell of his ranch house is still on the flatlands just below the St. Mary's Dam spillway on the southeast portion of the Kainai Nation. The barn is

Garry Allison Photo

Neighbour Harley Frank stands in front of old Three Persons' ranch house

gone; just a pile of old sun-greyed siding remains. But the memories of the first Indian world champion saddle bronc rider are still vivid in the minds of the Kainai people.

Indian athletes have always laboured under a pall and have been forced to become over-achievers in order to break even. Many have become not only people I am proud to know, but lifelong friends.

Look among these athletes and you will find many have become among the best in Canada, but some have risen to world championship levels. It has been an honour for me to know and work among these renowned athletes.

Rodeo Legends

Ever since Bill Wright, an older cousin, took me to my first rodeo as a five-year-old - the same age I saw my first Calgary Stampede while staying in the cowtown with my aunt and uncle - I have been a fan of the sport. It was Bill who took me along to Stan Walker's house, and I even helped on the hay rake, as we did Stan's field. I was sitting right on the arena fence when he won the steer decorating at Calgary, and as he walked back to the chutes, he said "Hi Kid." I was in heaven.

As the years passed I attended professional, amateur, high school and IRCA rodeos - literally hundreds of them. I've come to know first generation cowboys and then their sons or daughters. Most of the people in rodeo are honest, straight-shooters, none more so than folks I deal with here.

Harold Mandeville

When a cowboy's days are done, you can generally judge his ability by the number of championships he has earned throughout his career. But more importantly you can judge the character of the man by the number of friends who gathered to honour his life when his career and life on this earth have drawn to a close.

Such was the case with Harold Mandeville. When the big cowboy passed away Sept. 19, 2008, the entire South Pavilion of Exhibition Park was filled beyond capacity with fellow cowboys, a slew of non-rodeo types, natives, politicians, family, friends and media to honour and celebrate the memory of this fine rodeo cowboy and man.

The mild-mannered, soft spoken Harold - who had trouble remembering names (that was one of his wife Pearl's duties) - left everyone he met with a feeling they were indeed important men or women in Harold's eyes. He had an

impact on his sport outside the rodeo arena - it was Harold and Pearl who created the Rodeo News, and who encouraged me, as a novice writer, to cover rodeos in the south and write-up the stories for their fledging newspaper - and close to 50 years later I'm still gushing forth.

For that reason, and many others, Harold Mandeville will always be my King of the Cowboys.

Harold Mandeville, was born in Manyberries, Alberta in 1925 and was raised in an equally small town called Skiff.

Harold was always modest, silent and talented, and a champion rodeo cowboy. A member of the Canadian Rodeo Hall of Fame, Harold was named rodeo's Cowboy of the Year in 1972 and dominated the sport during his active rodeoing days.

From 1946 to 1973 - quite a span when you think about it - Harold won eight major Canadian rodeo championships and placed in the top five in steer wrestling/decorating, bareback bronc riding and bull riding, as well as calf roping nine other times. In 1946 he won the steer decorating crown, where a ribbon was slipped onto the steer's horn at full gallop from the back of a horse. The event gave way to steer wrestling.

Besides his 1946 steer decorating title Harold was all around champion in 1965, bareback king in 1947, calf roping champion in 1960 - an event he came to late in life - and in 1947, 1952, 1957 and 1966 he was the steer wrestling champion. As well, he was the all-around champion and steer decorating king at the Calgary Stampede in 1951 and 1957 respectively.

"I imagine I liked steer wrestling the best of all the events," Harold said. "That and the decorating were my events at the time, I had done them ever since I started. I would have liked calf roping just as well too, if I had started out with it."

He didn't throw his first rope in a rodeo arena until he was 34 years of age. But he was still good enough at it to be the Canadian champion in 1960. Harold never did compete as an amateur, he learned his trade at Canadian pro rodeos. He also built an indoor roping and steer wrestling arena on his farm just west of Lethbridge to practice in, the first of its kind. It was there he learned to calf rope.

"Harold used to get off the right side when he roped, the only cowboy around southern Alberta at that time who did that. He didn't have to duck under his rope and he was in good position to flank his calf coming off the right side," said wife Pearl. Today, virtually every calf roper dismounts on the right side.

He rode bulls, but not much after he married his wife Pearl on November 15, 1952 at Great Falls, Montana, and never rode bulls again after 1955 when daughter Vicki was born. "People used to say I made him quit riding, but I didn't," Pearl said. "I even used to enter him in the bull riding and bareback events at rodeos."

Harold's first professional rodeo was in Picture Butte in 1946, where he thinks he won something but can't really recall. He thinks he won something because a cowboy at the following rodeo in Fort Macleod offered to lend him his horse after he'd turned Harold down in Picture Butte. His final rodeo is also something Harold couldn't quite recall. It was either Regina or Brandon, in 1973.

"I think it was Regina," he said. "I really wasn't going to quit, just slow down. I sold the horse I was using to Jim Gladstone. I had another I was going to use, but it died. I just never started out again."

The Mandevilles have a son Bryan and daughters Vicki and Cathy, who lives in Australia.

During his rodeo days Harold used to travel with Bob Duce, Reg Kesler, Carol Olsen and at times Stan Walker and Bud Vancleave. Harold was usually the designated driver, after all most of the time it was his car. "I went where they wanted to go, I was just starting and they were the veterans so I figured they knew what they were doing," Harold said with a laugh. "We had quite a time."

When Harold showed up at one of his first rodeos in Shelby, Montana in 1945 he planned on decorating a steer and then riding a steer. Instead he was faced with two new events, steer wrestling and bull riding. For both the decorating and the dogging he'd often use one of the Butterfield brothers' horses and at other times he used Stan Walker's team.

"Back then there were no bulls, you rode steers. Around southern Alberta it was the Ring Brothers who brought in the first real bulls, those big Brahmas, to ride. Calgary and High River, which the Burtons contracted, had cross-bred bulls, but the ordinary rodeos used native steers. The steers weren't as rank or mean as the bulls were - they wouldn't fight you like the bulls. My problem was I didn't know how to get off them when the ride was over, that's why I got hurt a lot."

Harold was a late starter in rodeo and was 21 when he entered his first show. He was also the oldest cowboy to win a Canadian all around championship, at age 40. During his rodeo career, from 1946 to 1973, Harold, late start or not, proved to be one of Canada's rodeo greats.

He is the only rodeo cowboy to have a span of 20 years between his first Canadian championship and his last. When it was all over he had won eight major championships, 13 trophy saddles and the C.N. Woodward Award as Canadian Cowboy of the Year. He's also in the Alberta and Lethbridge Sports Halls of Fame and Canadian Rodeo Hall of Fame.

He competed in virtually every rodeo event,

Mandeville Family Photo
Pearl Mandeville and her favourite horse

82

with the exception of saddle bronc riding. "I got on a couple of saddle broncs, but I got bucked off so fast I never bothered trying them again," said the man who was influenced in his early rodeo career by the Lund family. "I wish now I would have given bronc riding an honest try, and also, I wish I'd started calf roping at an earlier age."

Harold and Pearl created the Canadian Rodeo News in 1964. "We printed two editions a month, out at Taber, and we sold our own ads and wrote the paper too," said Pearl, a top barrel racer in her day. Ads in the Mandeville's Canadian Rodeo News were $2 a column inch, 10 cents a word in the classified, and $140 for a full page. The paper did have the backing of the Canadian Professional Rodeo Cowboys Association right from the start, with the pro office owning 25 per cent of the newspaper.

The Mandevilles operated the paper for four years, developing it into a great success. Then the CPRA decided they wanted it all. "They wanted it," Pearl said. "Harold had always wanted to be around rodeo in some way after he retired and that's why we started the paper. Then they bought it."

Harold was quite upset about being pressured into selling, but he finally mellowed. "I now know it's better up there (at the CPRA office in Calgary) and I guess now I'm glad they have it," he said.

One of the highlights for Pearl came when Reg Kesler named one of his top broncs Rodeo News, after the Mandeville's newspaper. The bronc went on to win a world championship.

Pearl remembers the rush to get the first issue out and the fact both she and Harold were suffering with pneumonia and were so sick a doctor had to make a house call. But they got the paper together and sent it out to the Taber Times to be printed.

The idea for the Rodeo News came when Pearl and Harold were heading home from the

Garry Allison Photo

Harold Mandeville with some of his many rodeo trophies

first Canadian Professional Rodeo in Toronto, back in November, 1963. The long ride gave them plenty of time to talk and they knew people would be asking them who won what down east. At first it was just talk of the rodeo between themselves, then the idea came to write a newsletter. "By the time we got to Regina the idea was more of a miniature newspaper," said Pearl. "Then we knew we had to create a newspaper."

The Mandevilles saw their newspaper as dealing with special news items in the sport, covering upcoming rodeos, and publishing the results of past rodeos. There would be standings, stories, barrel racing news, profiles and who knows what else in their newspaper.

The pair presented their proposal to the CPRA and the Association came on board for 25 per cent of the business. The association agreed it would supply the results and any other up-to-the-minute facts it felt were relevant.

Despite being advised against the venture by experts, the couple started the Canadian Rodeo News, backed by $3,000 in guaranteed notes in the bank. A mailing list was put together and when the rodeo season rolled around in 1964 the Rodeo News was also ready to roll.

The first edition was eight pages and included coverage of the Toronto rodeo. The presses ran off 2,500 issues and the paper was sold through subscription and at booths at the rodeos, with free copies stuck on windshields at the Edmonton rodeo - but it rained.

The final issue for the Mandevilles was December 16, 1967. But the foundation they laid continues to flourish as the Canadian Rodeo News.

Pearl was known in barrel racing circles as the classiest dresser around, besides being a tough competitor. She was so interested in her sport she even brought world champion Ardith Bruce to town to put on a clinic on the do's and don'ts of barrel racing.

I dropped out to the Rainbow Indoor Riding Arena for a day, not to barrel race but to meet Bruce. I remember her telling the girls on hand there were two important factors in racing: one, make sure your hat had enough bobbie pins in it to stay on your head; and two, put elastic bands around your boots and stirrups to keep your foot from bouncing loose as you wildly kicked your horse on the home stretch.

Malcolm Jones

They called him Rip, and it sure wasn't for his outgoing mannerisms. Malcolm Jones, despite making a name as one of the best bareback bronc riders in the world, was anything but bubbly. Quiet and laid back, Malcolm attended the LCI at the same time I did and we've known each other for quite some time after he left school, though it was his brother Allan - the exact opposite of Malcolm - whom I was more familiar with. Then Malcolm started bronc riding at the same time I was covering sports for The Lethbridge Herald, and boy, was he ever one of the best. We shared one other great moment, when we were both inducted into the Lethbridge Sports Hall of Fame the same night. I felt good going at the same time as such a great athlete.

Everything is all right if you are having fun. And Malcolm Jones had fun.

"I enjoyed riding bareback broncs, it was physically challenging but I had fun riding them," said Malcolm, just a few weeks before his induction into Canada's Professional Rodeo Hall of Fame. "It was only later, after 13 years of it,

Garry Allison Photo

Malcolm Jones, a Canadian bareback legend

that I started to get tired. The travel killed me, it got so I just didn't want to go any more.

"I went to Medicine Hat in 1971 from the home farm at Vauxhall and I had to get on Reg Kesler's bronc, Three Bars, one of the best. When I got there I found I'd left my rigging bag at home. That's when I decided it was time to quit, my mind just wasn't on it any more."

As it was, with a borrowed rigging, Malcolm climbed aboard Three Bars and placed fifth. It was the last ride for the Canadian champion, and if you had checked the crowd most would have predicted both Malcolm and Three Bars would wind up in the Hall of Fame someday; and they have.

Like any Canadian riding bareback broncs in the 1960s and 1970s, Malcolm and Three Bars teamed up more than a few times, as did Malcolm and Moonshine, another top Kesler bareback bronc in the Hall of Fame.

The soft-spoken Malcolm was never afraid of Three Bars, though many top hands were.

"Three Bars was probably the strongest bareback horse there was, along with Harry Vold's Necklace. They were the two most powerful barebacks in the world. They could let you down any time. I drew Three Bars once at Brooks and she threw me off harder than any horse, ever. Three Bars had plenty of mallards (ducks) in her. If you got past the third jump you were often okay, but you could still be in real trouble.

"I liked riding Moonshine, I never bucked off him. He was one of my favourite broncs to get on," Jones recalled.

One of Malcolm' most disheartening rides came aboard Moonshine. He'd turned in a sparkling performance on the world and Canadian champion bronc and seemed certain to win the Calgary Stampede - before the $50,000 ride-off - but a judge claimed he slapped the bronc, an almost unheard of thing in bareback riding except when a rider is pulled forward and is in trouble. Malcolm was goose-egged. Repeated replays on television showed Malcolm was no where close to slapping the bronc, but it was too late.

Malcolm never did win Calgary, despite a number of trips to the finals, in both bareback and saddle bronc riding.

"All these years later I still know there's no way I slapped that horse," Malcolm said quietly.

"I was jobbed. Winning Calgary was a pretty important part of your life then, it not only involved Calgary but included a Charlie Biel bronze as well."

Moonshine, Three Bars and Necklace were the bareback broncs who challenged Malcolm's abilities to the fullest, with one other possible exception, a Calgary Stampede bronc called Tuffy, who also showed up at a lot of Kesler rodeos.

During his 13 years in the sport Malcolm Jones won four Canadian bareback titles, was runner-up in the all-around race once, and second for a fifth bareback crown by a mere $41. On the world scene he placed as high as third, missing the silver buckle by a mere $3,500.

"When you think back you always think, 'well, if I just went to a few more rodeos; if I'd rodeoed more in the eastern United States; if I'd have stayed in the U.S. . . . or I should have tried harder,'" said Malcolm. "It is all second guessing now, and a lot of ifs, but really it came down to the travel thing."

Malcolm was in Little Rock, Arkansas, during his biggest year, 1965, tired, worn out, home sick and resting in the shade at the back of the chutes. He'd been going steady for quite some time. "I asked myself, 'what am I doing here?' and I got up, said goodbye and drove straight through to the farm at Vauxhall. I stayed there three weeks, and the others kept on going, chasing that buckle."

Jim Houston of Omaha, Nebraska won it. Malcolm's three-week holiday left him in third, $3,500 behind.

A high school principal is supposed to guide his students into suitable occupations. That is exactly what Lethbridge Collegiate Principal D.S.A. Kyle did with a young Grade 11 student in 1959. "He called me into his office and asked me to make up my mind, either go rodeoing or go to school," said Malcolm. "He told me I wasn't doing anything in school except taking up space . . . so I decided to go rodeoing." The decision to follow the rodeo trail proved to be insightful on both Malcolm's and Kyle's part.

Malcolm, born in Lethbridge in 1940, was raised in Vauxhall until the family moved to Taber when he was 10. He remained in Taber until his Grade 9 year when the family finally settled in Lethbridge. Two years later, upon

Malcolm Jones on the great Reg Kesler bronc Moonshine at the Medicine Hat Stampede

receiving the D.S.A. Kyle directive, Malcolm left high school. One of the first things he did was go to work for another Canadian rodeo great, and also a Hall of Fame member, Harold Mandeville. While honing his skills as a farmer and cattleman with Mandeville, Malcolm ran into Gordie Ross, son of Salty Ross, a pioneer rodeo cowboy.

The pair, Ross and Malcolm, went rodeoing. They threw a mattress on the roof of a 1953 Chev and headed for Saskatchewan - Clear Water Lake, Jack Kiss Lake, Moose Jaw. Then they moved into northern Alberta, to Bruce, Rimbey and a few other amateur shows.

"We did quite well," said Malcolm with a small, satisfied grin. We won some money in bareback and saddle bronc, and came home with about $500, a lot of money back then."

That winter Malcolm worked for Mike Aldof in his saddle shop, which once stood in what today is the Sandman Inn mini-mall. He worked with an old rodeo cowboy, and expert saddle

maker, Bud Sharpee. But Bud wanted to take in a few winter rodeos in the southern United States, and he talked Malcolm and another new kid, Kenny McLean, into going along.

Come February, they loaded up and headed for Arizona, Malcolm applying for the Professional Rodeo Cowboys Association card even before he had a Canadian card. The trio teamed with three other American cowboys and rented a house in Wickenberg, Arizona, using it as a home base. All Malcolm picked up was experience, no cash. He returned home, borrowed some money to go into Saskatchewan to rodeo, and came back even broker.

"I started to wonder what I was doing," said Malcolm.

By spring 1961 he was working for wages in the oil patch, on a seismic crew. Despite the money being good and the work being steady, he decided to give rodeo one more shot. He has never looked back. From 1961, through to his

86

retirement in 1971, Malcolm never finished lower than fourth in the Canadian bareback standings. He concentrated on bareback broncs, but rode saddle broncs and enjoyed steer wrestling later in his career

"Bareback riding seemed to match my attitude . . . it's kind of wild. I kind of had a don't give a damn attitude back then and you had to have that to ride bareback broncs."

From his first major professional win at Vancouver in 1961, when he won a go-round, Malcolm knew he made the right decision when he talked to the LCI principal.

"That Vancouver money was a big win and quite a thrill," Malcolm said.

And from there, success just kept building.

Rodeo today has a lot more money up for grabs than it did 55 years ago when a young Malcolm hit the trail. But, with the rise in purse money, came a rise in expenses as well, so the cowboy still isn't making the big bucks of the major sports he said.

"I could buy a new Oldsmobile for about $3,500 and hit the road back then, but today that same car is about $35,000," said Malcolm.

Also among the changes to the sport is the way rodeo is conducted.

When Malcolm and his carload of friends arrived for a rodeo, likely as not they stayed around for a day or two because there were probably two go-rounds and a finals.

"Now the cowboys enter 10 rodeos and go to three," the former Canadian Professional Rodeo Cowboys Association president said. "In my day you only entered the rodeos you could get to. Today, there are turnouts every time you turn around. I see it happening on the amateur circuit too. They'll have six bareback riders entered and only three will show up.

"With the pros, I can understand the economics, but they shouldn't do it. All the top professional guys want to make the National Finals Rodeo, that's their big payday."

Malcolm qualified for the NFR four times. All he had at year's end were the leftovers from paying his bills, a pocket full of gas stubs and a worn out new car. Plus, he was tired. But any money earned at the NFR was gravy.

"After I got over chasing the buckle (the silver and gold world championship buckle) I'd just go to rodeos I wanted to and get on," Malcolm said. "Then, I started to clear around $10,000 a year. I wasn't chasing the buckle all over North America, I was staying around home and I was better off by far, money wise."

Malcolm rode bareback and saddle broncs, but he never went after the saddle broncs with the gusto he used for the bareback event. However, he was number four in Canada once in the saddle bronc riding. He didn't like the required spurring motion of the saddle broncs, it took all the skin off his legs hitting the swells of the saddle he said with a laugh.

"The only time I was ever hurt in the chutes was on a saddle bronc. It fell back over on me. When you are set in that saddle there's not much chance of getting out, you're going over with the horse. That's the real bad part of saddle bronc riding, the action in the chutes," recalled Jones.

He also tried his hand at bull dogging, taking it up seriously after one winter in the United States when he was staying with C.R. Boucher, the 1964 world steer wrestling champion, and top-ranked Dewey Dunaway. They had more than 200 head of practice steers and the pair of champions taught Malcolm how to bulldog. They started him on the ground, teaching him how to set his feet out in front of him by setting up a rig on the side of a pick-up truck and driving around the arena. Then he began standing in front of the chutes and grabbing the steer on the way out.

"Finally I was on a horse," he said with a smile. "I played with those boys for about three weeks. I did all right at bulldogging and I came that close to the all-around championship in Canada in 1969, finishing second to Kenny Maclean but ahead of Tom Bews."

Malcolm turned to the political side of rodeo in 1970-1971 as president of the CPRA. It was during his tenure Canadian rodeo made a giant stride, creating the Canadian Finals Rodeo. Though Malcolm wasn't president the year the sudden-death finals began, it was during his presidency the package was put in place for the CFR. He liked the sudden-death aspect of the early days of the CFR.

"It took all the pressure off guys going down the road to finish first for the year," he said. "You just don't do well financially that way, chasing the buckle all year. With the sudden-death aspect you just have to make the top 10 to have a crack at the buckle and a lot of cash as well.

Going into the Canadian Rodeo Hall of Fame officially put Malcolm among the rodeo elite.

"It was tremendous," Malcolm said of his induction into the Hall. "The importance of it began to hit home a few weeks after being named. I began to realize only a selected few get to go in. I got singled out, so I must have accomplished something special. My family is very proud of this whole thing. It's very special. So many other people could be in there too, and you wonder, `why me?'"

Here's why: Malcolm Jones, in 13 years as a professional, won 17 trophy saddles, more than 40 silver buckles and a like number of trophies. His Canadian championships came in 1963, 1964, 1966 and 1967. He won the Houston Livestock Show's bareback bronc riding, was in the Finals at the Calgary Stampede in both the bareback and saddle bronc events a number of times, qualified for four National Finals Rodeo appearances and set a NFR bareback record of 186 points under the old 200-point scoring system. He won a raft of trophy saddles on the old Southern Circuit and won his hometown rodeo at Lethbridge at least three times. He missed a fifth Canadian bareback crown by a mere $41 to Dale "Trapper" Trottier and was second in the all around race in 1969.

The first Canadian bareback bronc rider to ever qualify for the NFR, Malcolm said he had some good times, and some sad times in rodeo.

"You made a lot of life-long friends, and while you may not see them too often any more, you are real glad to see them again," he said. "There's a real bond there."

Among his friends were C.N. Chunky Woodward and Ted Vayro, with the three of them forming Grasslands Rodeo Co. upon Malcolm's retirement from competition.

Malcolm enjoyed rodeo, though he found the travel gruelling. The high price of constant highway travel impacted Malcolm in another way as well, when he saw friends like Dick Nash and Bob Duce die in car wrecks. "I had breakfast with Bob, and that night he was dead," Malcolm said in a low, somber tone. "He was probably the greatest bareback bronc rider to come out of Canada. One year he went to 17 straight U.S. rodeos and won them all. Dick was a saddle bronc rider and we stayed together. He left one morning for a rodeo and two hours later was dead. These things impact you more than a little."

If the road and riding broncs was gruelling, Malcolm found stock contracting was an equally tough haul.

"The third year Chunky, Ted and I were together we had every rodeo in B.C., pro and amateur, from Prince George south," said Malcolm. "At the end of the year you finish up looking for feed and covering the cost of mileage. After all those months on the road, we had $5,000 in our account, and still had to have feed for the winter. When I got married I walked away from rodeo, but I was still part owner of Grasslands for a few years after. I got out simply because it was a matter of economics. You'd start out each spring with a big debt and work to pay it back all summer, just to get even so you could start all over again."

Malcolm waited until he left rodeo to marry wife Carol, from Irvine, Alberta in 1974. They have two children, Dayne and Jo Lien.

In his later years he turned to operating a 900-acre irrigation farm and leases "a lot of dry grass" through the Vauxhall Grazing Association, for his 120 head of cows. Once away from rodeo he became involved in the community and is a past-chairman of the Vauxhall Grazing Association and the Southern Alberta Grazing Association and he sits on the appeal board for the Municipal District of Taber.

While Malcolm Jones' rodeo days are behind him they still mean a lot, through friends made, honours earned, good times, special memories and the induction into Canada's Pro Rodeo Hall of Fame.

Herman Linder

I knew Herman Linder for many decades. He was a man who lived with his notoriety. He loved to talk about rodeo, past and present and he loved to talk about his ranch, in the low foothills south and east of Cardston. He drove me around the ranch one day, up the back hills, along the fence line and we stopped atop a hill. You could see the prairies in one direction, the mountains in another, dominated by old Chief, north to Cardston and south into the United States.

Herman was a character, the last of a breed. Coming out from his funeral and standing in front of the LDS Church in Cardston - another idiosyncrasy of his was to tell new acquaintances he was the Bishop of Cardston, which he wasn't, far from it - you saw a true cross-section of people, both in age and interest.

Herman touched a lot of lives. I wrote a lot about Herman through the years, dating back to the late 1970s and as late as 2000.

"If I felt any better I'd have a runway." That's how a 91-year-old Herman Linder, one of the world's great rodeo cowboys, received the news that he had been named a Member of the Order of Canada. The Order of Canada is bestowed on Canadians who have attained outstanding achievements and made significant contributions during their lifetime. Members are selected from all segments of Canadian Society and Herman became the first rodeo cowboy named to this high honour.

"This is something I never ever dreamed of happening," Herman said. "I must be dreaming, it can't be true, but I feel quite proud. I just hope I don't wake up and find I was dreaming. All these other cowboys deserve the same thing, you know."

The mention of Herman Linder's name in rodeo and ranching circles from Edmonton to El Paso and Vancouver to Montreal brought instant recognition. He'd been a friend of politicians, like John Diefenbaker, Joey Smallwood and Senator Joyce Fairbairn, and an acquaintance of Queen Elizabeth II. He was a friend of Kainai Chief Jim Shot Both Sides, cattlemen like the late Dick Gray and athletes like Fritzie Hansen.

Through the years Herman came to know them all, from rodeo greats like Casey Tibbs, Pete Knight and the Canada Kid, to recording and film stars like Slim Pickens, Wilf Carter, Rod Cameron, Rex Allen, Guy Weadick and lifelong friend Gene Autry.

Herman's world encompassed everything from bucking horses to ballroom dancing. Herman's waltzing was done in Vienna during a visit to the city immortalized by Strauss, but he also waltzed broncs around the rodeo arenas of North America, Australia and Europe. He related stories of his Vienna trip as casually as he recalled the horseback parade down Broadway each year, with chuckwagons, floats and ticker tape. When the pro rodeo moved into Madison Square Garden in New York, cowboys would parade through the city each year to be welcomed on the steps of city hall by the mayor.

Herman's den walls were covered, literally floor to ceiling, with photos of friends and with awards. His awards and achievements, not only in rodeo but in business and social circles, were staggering.

He was a member of the Kainai Chieftainship, given the name Calf Shirt; was a member of Rodeo Halls of Fame in the United States and Canada; he earned Alberta's Master Farm Family award winner in 1971; the Alberta Maine-Anjou Man of the Year; and was the Rangeman of the Year during the 66th Oldtimers Rangemen's Dinner at the Palliser Hotel in Calgary during the Calgary Stampede. And speaking of the Stampede, Herman held more Calgary championships than any other cowboy, past or present.

He was a member of the Lethbridge and District Exhibition Hall of Fame; the Alberta

Herman Linder was arena director for many top rodeos with his friend Reg Kesler, including this one in Fort Macleod

89

Sports Hall of Fame; and a life and honourary member of stampede boards, Rotary clubs and other organizations. He was named Cardston and district's Male Athlete of the century in 1987. In 1996 he received a silver belt buckle during the Cowboy's reunion at the National Finals Rodeo in Las Vegas - Herman never missed attending a National Finals Rodeo until ill health got in the way late in his life.

His old friend Harold Gunderson has written his story in *The Linder Legend: The Story of Pro Rodeo and its Champion*. Much of the material in that book was gleaned from diaries Herman faithfully kept through the years.

Herman's rodeo career was relatively short, about 10 years, but it was brilliant. He said in those early days of rodeo, in the late 1920s and early 1930s saddle bronc riding was the premier event. Despite that, scores weren't announced to the crowds and even the draw for broncs prior to the rodeo was a secret. One of the first rodeos to post the rider's score or time on a scoreboard was at Edmonton.

"The rodeos didn't all have bull riding and bareback riding in those early times," said Herman. "These boys today have no idea what a gravy train they've got." Herman recalled one stock contractor, Leo Cranmer, who used to pay $5 mount money to bull riders - and even when bull riding was part of the rodeo he'd only put up $15, $10 and $5 in prize money.

"In those days the bares and bulls were not up with the saddle broncs, the steer decorating or calf roping events. It's a lot different today."

No one dominated the Calgary Stampede the way Herman Linder did, from 1929 through 1938. He took home 22 Calgary Stampede trophies in a nine-year period, more than any other cowboy has ever won. "Back then it was just an honour to say you even rode at the Calgary Stampede," he said.

From his relatively humble beginnings to his achievements as one of the great rodeo legends of all time, Herman always remained a man of the people. Herman loved to talk and he frequented rodeos, socials and cattle events almost to the very end.

He enjoyed the best, flew high and fast during the good times and lived a rough, busy, fulfilling life. But he also saw the down side. He lost his brother Warner in 1983, his first wife Agnes in 1985 and son George in a farm accident a year later. He'd been injured as a cowboy, nearly killed as a rodeo director and had been hurt working on the ranch. But he always bounced back.

Herman and his second wife Adeline, whom he married May 26, 1990, lived in the cozy ranch house he built in 1939 on the Linder Ranch within a few dozen metres of the old log cabin he and Agnes began their lives together.

Herman was a happy man, still living in the old house built in 1939 on the Linder Ranch right up to his passing. Next to the old log house he and Agnes started in was the sprawling new home of the ranch's new owners, Brad and Lydia Beazer and their family.

Herman's Calgary Stampede Titles

1929 - Bareback bronc champion
        Canadian saddle bronc champion
1931 - Canadian all-around champion
1932 - North American all-around
                champion
        Canadian all-around champion
1933 - Canadian all-around champion
1934 - Bareback bronc champion
        Bull riding champion
        Canadian saddle bronc champion
        Canadian all-around champion
        North American all-around champion

1935 - Bull riding champion
        Canadian all-around champion
        North American all-around champion
1936 - Bareback bronc champion
        Bull riding champion
        Canadian all-around champion
        North-American all-around champion
1938 - Bull riding champion
        Canadian saddle bronc champion
        Canadian all-around champion
        North American all-around champion

"Brad told me I could live there for the next 10 years when I sold him the ranch," said Herman. "I still have eight years to go, but Brad told me I could stay on even longer it I wanted too.

"If son George hadn't passed away . . . Well, I always thought the Linder Ranch would go on forever. Daughter Rosemarie and Tom Bews have their own ranch. Their boys are busy with that, working in the movies and with rodeo too. So I sold."

The first time he rode in a rodeo, Herman Linder was only 14 . . . and he was dressed as a girl. "They gave me $6, which in those days was pretty good money," said Herman with a big smile. "In those days (mid-1920s) you got mount money, $1 to ride a steer and $3 for a bronc. I got $6 to ride dressed as a girl. It was great money. When I got back behind the chutes I couldn't get that dress off fast enough though."

His first win at a rodeo came at age 16 on a bronc called Yellow Fever, when he tied with Tommy Wells. After switching horses for a re-ride, the judges declared both men should split the first-place prize of $35. One of the rodeoing Lund boys finished second. Due to the rules of the time, with the other two splitting first with $17.50 each, Lund took home more money, $22, for finishing second.

The first time Herman was in with the "big" names of the day - the cowboys like Canada Kid and Pete Knight - was at High River in 1929, the real start to his short but successful rodeo career.

"That was the first time I was in with the wolves," he said with his distinctive laugh. "I won first in the day money in bareback and saddle bronc riding and won the average in bareback. I never dreamed I would go on the world rodeo trail."

From that year through 1939, with one year virtually missing due to injury, Herman would dominate the Calgary Stampede.

Herman was born in Wisconsin and arrived in the Cardston district in 1918, as a 10-year-old.

"We came by train, up through Portal, Sask., and we stayed at the Cahoon Hotel when we got to Cardston. There were no cars around, but I could see lots of horses and wagons on main street and thought 'boy, this will be great.'"

Two years later he saw his first rodeo, a little bronc riding exhibition during a baseball game at

A portion of Linder's 1000 acre ranch

Aetna. Each guy brought his own bronc to ride and one of the riders was a Woolf, brother of the great jockey George 'The Iceman' Woolf, born and raised in Cardston. Herman was impressed with what he saw. So he decided to give it a try.

Sometime in 1920 he put a saddle on a yearling heifer. The animal jumped this way and that, but the young Herman stayed aboard. After seeing a rodeo at Cardston he developed a bareback rigging, rivetted it together, and tried it on a neighbour's bronc at home.

"I'll never forget it, I was only about 14 and it was January or February. We had no buck chutes and a neighbour had some horses, one of them about 1,400 pounds. We snubbed it tight against a post, my brother Warner and me. Warner helped me on and he turned him loose.

"I rode that doggone horse and eventually it started running. I don't remember how long that horse ran, but it finally slowed down a bit and I eventually stepped off him. My Dad had no idea what was going on and if he did he probably would have been against it. It was a wonder we weren't all killed with some of the things we did as kids. I am firmly convinced you are born to do some things, and bronc riding for me, well, it just came natural."

After a brief but illustrious 10 year career he had decided to retire during the 1939 season when he was 31, feeling that by the time he reached 32 he'd be on the down side of what had been a great career. He rode for the last time in Lewiston, Idaho and won. Then he ended his career by fulfilling a goal, to return to New York's Madison Square Garden, where some of his most impressive wins were recorded, to judge the great Garden Rodeo.

"When you reach age 32 in most sports

there's only one way you're going to go. In 1938 I decided it would be nice to rodeo one more year because we'd saved enough to build a home. Most cowboys have had enough after 10 years (especially competing in five events) - the injuries weaken you. A human is like a machine - the harder they're used, the quicker they wear out."

Herman climaxed his career by judging at Madison Square Garden, the fulfilment of a dream. He judged at the impressive Garden and then returned home to Cardston, never to ride another saddle bronc. He did rope a few calves, but Herman never worked the rough stock events again.

"I darn near went crazy that winter - a guy quitting dope couldn't go through the hell that I did that first winter. I was like a caged animal. I'm sure if I hadn't told so many people I don't know if I could have stood it. There I was at home and all my friends were still on the road rodeoing."

From there, Herman went on to judge a few other rodeos, then produce rodeos from Montreal's Expo 67 to Vancouver. He set up the Southern Circuit, a selection of the best rodeos in southern Alberta, before being retired by a near-fatal arena accident in Fort Macleod's Midnight Stadium.

In 1983 Herman said the key to a financially successful rodeo career was a little black book. Agnes Linder said, during husband Herman's rodeo life, she carried a little black book and kept track of "absolutely everything," from five cent chocolate bars to hotel expenses. She accompanied her husband to all the rodeos he competed in during the 1930s, from Australia to Madison Square Garden to Lethbridge. The only trip she didn't make was to England.

"Our rodeo life was a little like a honeymoon," Agnes said. "We went to all the rodeos together, it wasn't that hard - and I kept my black book - that's an easy way to save money. A lot of the cowboys, then and now, liked to party, but we never did. I didn't go to England because it was either that or get a new cook stove.

Pearl Mandeville Photo
Tom Bews, Linder's son-in-law

The stove won out."

When the Linders celebrated their 50th wedding anniversary Agnes remembered her drive to the Linder ranch only a few days after they were married, on a bitter, cold New Year's Eve.

The old Chrysler they were driving got stuck in the snow and a neighbour had to harness his team and pull the newlyweds home. She said the two-roomed Linder home was crowded, with a curtain across one room separating Herman and Agnes from Herman's parents – his brother Warner slept in the kitchen.

"Times were hard in those early days. We even had the telephone taken out because we couldn't afford the $1.50," Agnes said.

"We had no radio, just a carry-all phonograph. Dad Linder was a good card player and we played bridge every night, with the school teacher joining us – the couple that sat out pulled wool for carding."

Agnes said she was "too green" to worry about Herman injuring himself in a rodeo arena in those early days.

She said she'd do it all again, mainly because of the friendships they built. Sitting with contestants' wives she soon learned not to judge and not to talk about anybody – so she'd sit and wouldn't say anything.

"I won't lie, I was Herman's worst critic and I still am," Agnes said. "Rodeo life then was what you wanted to make it – there were both sides of life."

Of all his accomplishments the one of which Herman felt particularly proud of was the part he played in the formation of the Cowboys Turtle Association, Oct. 30, 1936 during a cowboy strike at the Boston Gardens. The Turtle Association was the forerunner of today's American and Canadian rodeo cowboy associations and gave the cowboys a say in the rodeo business.

On his wall hung the original document, stating "We the undersigned demand that the purses be doubled and the entrance fees added in each and every event." The undersigned names include Canada Kid (Lee Farris), Dusty Vaughn,

Joe Wolf, Dick Truitt, Pete Knight and, of course, Herman Linder who was the key organizer of the entire movement.

Through all his years in rodeo Herman saw the best, among them his son-in-law Tom Bews who won numerous Canadian all-around and saddle bronc titles. Herman was reluctant to single out the greats he'd seen, but he did name a few.

In selecting stock he said there's been so many changes in the sport through the years, but saddle broncs like Five Minutes To Midnight, Midnight and Hell's Angel were unbeatable when they were at their best.

"In my book I say the best bronc rider was Peter Knight. My God, when he was in his prime! . . . There were a lot of good ones through the years. Casey Tibbs was a tremendous rider and a tremendous guy too. There have been some tremendous bull riders too; Smokey Snyder was pretty hard to beat. He was born in Cardston you know. Dick Griffith was tremendous too.

"Slim Pickens worked as a clown for me for many years. He was a tremendous clown, just being funny or fighting the bulls."

Herman rodeoed on four continents, he rode against the best and produced rodeos with the best. He knew the best and was considered by all to be one of the best. In fact he said his life had been like a fairy tale. "If they had a Cinderella cowboy I'd qualify," he said with a laugh.

Herman travelled the world and earned enough money to build and furnish his home and establish himself on the Linder Ranch. The 1,600-acre spread ran 300 head of calves and 150 Maine Anjou cows and was operated by Herman's son George until his sudden, tragic death.

Time was though, from 1932 to 1939, Herman and Agnes, living in their 4x8 metre log cabin, had it rough. "I don't know how old that log house is but it was old when my folks moved here in 1918. We hit it pretty rough then. It was the midst of a dry spell – 1918 was the worst – and it broke most of the ranchers. We were poorer than broke. If my folks would have had their wish they couldn't have wished for anything that's half as good as we have now – we've got water in the corrals, electricity, gas, TV, cars and trucks."

Herman said the log house had an interesting history. He remembered when the Aetna school was burned Christmas day, putting students and the "school marm" and her family out into the cold. Another shack was found for the school, where students sat around a regular kitchen table, but the teacher needed a place to stay. Herman said there were six people living in his parents' two-roomed shack, along with the teacher and family, five in all, who moved into the log house.

"I went to Grade 8 and 9 in that log house, as well as church. It was bought from an outlaw originally - so it has seen everything, school, church, good, bad and families."

The Linders moved into their new home in 1939, bought with Herman's rodeo earnings when he retired. The log house remained on the Linder ranch, tucked away in the yard, a constant reminder of tougher times and of the Cinderella story that's Herman Linder's.

In 1971 Herman was honoured by the Southern Alberta Rodeo Circuit, an organization he helped found nearly 25 years previous. The Linders were also named an Alberta Master Farm Family, receiving a $1,000 cash award, a plaque and a special gate sign. One of the purposes of the master farmer award is to honour farm families who have excelled in farming, homemaking and citizenship, and to emphasize the advantages of farm life.

"Anyone can win a trophy, but the things people give you, the plaques and other awards,

Calgary Stampede Photo
This 3x3 foot signed photo of Herman on a bull at the Calgary Stampede was in my home for many years before I donated it to the Alberta Sports Hall of Fame

mean more," Herman once said. "Money can't buy that kind of thing."

Throughout his career Herman remained relatively free of injury in the rodeo arena. However, he received serious injuries when trampled by a horse at the Fort Macleod Stampede just prior to leaving for Expo in 1967. He came close to dying after a pick-up horse broadsided him in the arena.

It may sound like something out of Dr. Seuss, but a horse called Ham What Am played a key role in Herman's career. He drew Ham What Am at the World's Fair rodeo in Chicago in 1933, before he'd made a name for himself and long before people thought of him as a future hall of famer.

"I was getting on Ham What Am when world champion Earl Thode walked by and told me to shorten my rein a bit - if he hadn't done that the bronc would have bucked me off," Herman said. That was the turning point in his rodeo life. He said riding Ham What Am gave him courage and recognition. From then on he started winning money at rodeos. Ham What Am was not the best bronc Linder ever rode, though. That honour goes to Pardner.

Pardner was the old black horse the Linder boys used to ride as kids in the corral at the Linder ranch and went on to become a great saddle bronc. Had Pardner started bucking earlier in its life he would have earned a reputation as large as that of Midnight's claimed Herman. Pardner, renamed School Boy Roe in New York after the baseball player, was 1,400 pounds and broken to ride.

Herman's brother Warner once rode the horse into Cardston to perform for rodeo producer Ray Knight. Pardner impressed Knight by bucking off three riders.

"In 1934 at a rodeo in England I tried Pardner and he flung me again,"

Herman said. "I drew him in Boston in 1938 and this time I got by him to win day money. I had ridden him once before at the ranch. Warner said Pardner never bucked harder in his life."

Pardner was bucked in Indianapolis, New York and Boston and was only ridden four times in 1935 when he was at least 15 years old.

"By 1949 he was 19 and was still one of the 10 best horses in W.T. Johnson's string. Imagine what he would have been like if he could have bucked when he was younger. He was the greatest bucking horse I ever saw."

Herman said his luckiest horse was Easy Money, a stout bronc weighing 1,600 pounds, who was easy money for Herman.

He still had the chaps and bucking rein he used while rodeoing, but his spurs were stolen some time ago. He also had the saddle he began riding with.

By his own admission Herman could talk about rodeo for weeks on end. Ask a question and the Canadian rodeo immortal would answer it – and six others before they'd been asked. The stories literally flowed, dealing with his 10 years of active competition in the world's roughest sport in rodeo arenas from Australia to Calgary and Vancouver to New York. Calgary was his biggest show but he also won championships at shows such as Madison Square Garden and other smaller rodeos, such as Lethbridge.

It was 1980 that tended to cap off his career, with induction into two halls of fame, the Alberta Sports Hall of Fame and the coup de grace, the Cowboy Hall of Fame in the United States. "Being inducted into the Alberta Sports Hall of Fame was just great as well," he said. "Most of all it was great that they acknowledged the sport of rodeo, more so than myself. Rodeo and I are now right in there with all those other greats in many, many other sports, and I

Herman Linder, Calgary Stampede record holder

feel that is wonderful, inasmuch as rodeo is usually not recognized as a sport by many in the media.

"I guess I can't help but say I'm very honoured by the Cowboy Hall of Fame ceremony; after all anyone can go out and win a championship, but this affects me differently, there really are no words to explain it. In one's twilight years, to be honoured like this I guess shows that the whole world must have thought you were pretty good."

Rodeo announcer, producer, and former Oklahoma Senator Clem McSpadden gave a stirring speech at the Oklahoma induction ceremony, which moved Herman. "I am the only cowboy in the hall with trophies from three different countries on display, so that makes me sort of unique - as well as being a Canadian," Herman said.

On display at the U.S. Rodeo Hall of Fame were a saddle Herman won in New York; two cups he won in Australia in 1936 and 1938; a 14-carat gold belt buckle from his North American all around championship at Calgary; a silver cigarette case presented by the Prince of Wales in recognition of his 1934 Canadian saddle bronc title; and a gold watch for winning the bronc riding at Lethbridge.

"People today don't realize that the Calgary Stampede was like the finals rodeos they now have – a win at Calgary meant a North American or Canadian championship," Herman said. "A sad thing is that I have a room full of trophies that the Canadian cowboys association today doesn't recognize. I tell Tom (Bews), holder of five Canadian all around championships, that it would be like 30 years down the line the association changes the rules and decides not to recognize all Tom's championships. I ask him if he thinks that's fair?

"When the Canadian cowboys organized they decided not to recognize past champions, and their championship lists begin in 1945. On the other hand, when the American cowboys broke away from the old IRAA in 1940, which was formed in 1929, they recognized all the past champions.

In those days the three big rodeos were Calgary, Salinas and Cheyenne, and 75 per cent of all the other rodeos were in California. A point system was set up for determining champions and a win at Calgary would wrap up a championship. I remember when Nate Walden of Strathmore won the bareback in Calgary and was the world champion under the point system, despite the fact it was his only win of the year!"

In Australia Herman said they had a form of team rodeo, a concept Calgary tried in the 1980s and one that Herman disliked - especially because amateur cowboys were involved. "When we went to Australia we worked as a team, with individual titles as well," Herman said. "What they did was total the score of each member of the four-man team, and the highest total won the team event. Both years I was there the Canadians won the saddle bronc riding. You could substitute for injured team members. One time Clark Lund was injured in the dogging prior to the rodeo - he got a horn through the wrist. So, I rode his broncs and Jack Wade of Helkirk dogged his steers. I actually finished first on my broncs and second overall riding Clark's."

Herman loved stories about old riding days, horses, people, towns or countries. And occasionally someone told a tale or two about him.

A long-time Linder cohort, the late Dick Gray of Lethbridge, used to laugh about the time he, Herman, and two other friends flew to Denver for the Denver Stock Show. "We had trouble with the flight along the way and arrived late and missed the first performance of rodeo," Gray laughed. "So we decided to stay up and play a little poker. We played through the night and had to hurry to catch the plane home the next day. It was a hell of a long way to go just for a private poke game – we never did get to the rodeo.

"Herman loved to play crib too, and he was not adverse to counting 15-2, 15-4 and two make eight. One time Herman and I and Reg Kesler were playing crib at my place and a neighbour came over to see what the fight was all about. . . he thought my wife and I were really going at it."

Herman remembered a time, after a rodeo in Whitehall, Mont., when he and three cohorts were strapped for a little cash and decided to raise some money picking potatoes in Wyoming. He and his buddies stayed at a farm for $1 a day room and board and went out picking spuds. After three hours, and uncountable bag loads, they decided to count up their pay and figure out how much they had made. It didn't take them long to pull up stakes when they realized, if they picked for another seven hours, at the same rate, they'd have enough money to pay their room and board.

There are stories about how $10 would do a rodeo cowboy for weeks, with hotel, meals and gas all taken into account, and tales of horse races and an emptying wine barrel that belonged to Herman's future father-in-law.

"Four of us, on the way to a rodeo, showed up at Agnes' place in North Dakota by surprise, and of course were invited to stay," Herman said. "One of the boys was Pete DeForest, who could have been the best bronc rider ever, but Pete liked to take the odd drink."

To condense the tale, it seems DeForest discovered the wine barrel in the basement and soon put a healthy dint in its contents before Herman and friends caught him and put a stop to it.

"We were up half the night catching him sneaking back down for another shot," Herman laughed. "But, to top it off, after we left the guys stopped the car and opened up the trunk – they had tossed out most of my clothes and filled my suitcase with quart sealers of Agnes' father's wine. Her father never did figure out how come his wine barrel had emptied so fast, and it wasn't until years later that I even told Agnes."

In January of 1983 Bus Murdoch put together a tribute night for Herman and close to 400 people attended. While a limited number were able to express their opinions publicly, many had private opinions about the man they had gathered to honour.

"If ever there was a man that deserved to be honoured, Herman's it," said Lethbridge Exhibition Board member Tony Perlich. "He is a real hero."

Ken Buxton of Claresholm, a long-time horseman and chuckwagon outrider, former world saddle bronc champion Winston Bruce, Indian rodeo greats Fred Gladstone and Rufus Goodstriker, Chinook Rodeo Association president Bob Wilson, steer wrestlers Tommy Ivins and Lee Phillips and past rodeo star Harold Mandeville were on hand.

Western sculptor Corne Martens of Coaldale remembered the time, in 1934 in Saskatchewan, when he saw a Calgary Stampede poster featuring Linder aboard Easy Money. "Talk about heroes," Corne said. "Some 30 odd years later, I was in the Calgary Stampede office and saw that poster again – I was starting to do bronzes for the best cowboys in the world at Calgary and seeing the poster at that time was a real thrill."

There was some disappointment expressed because entertainers Slim Pickens and Rex Allen failed to appear. It was learned later that Pickens was dying of a brain tumour.

Lethbridge Mayor Andy Anderson opened the evening with a faux pas, praising Taber for holding the first pro rodeo in Canada. The honour belongs to Raymond, of course.

Master of ceremonies Dalton Elton entertained with three songs built around Herman's career and trick roper and cowboy movie star Montie Montana climbed up on the headtable for some rope tricks, culminating with a loop around Herman and wife Agnes.

There was more toasting than roasting during the evening. An oil painting by Larry Christensen, depicting Herman aboard a saddle bronc called Easy Money, with Chief Mountain in the background, sold for $3,000 to Lee Phillips, president of the Canadian Professional Rodeo Association. He also spent $1,700 for a larger, back-lit print of the same picture. A second lighted print was purchased by Fort Macleod Auction Market for $1,100.

"We bought the picture because we really feel Herman has done more for our cowboys than any other person we know of," Phillips said of the man who helped organize Cowboys Turtle Association, a forerunner of CPRA. "We'd be totally wrong not to honour Herman any way we can."

"What can I say? I am completely over-whelmed," Herman told the crowd. "Usually people wait until you're dead and gone before something like this – I keep pinching myself to see if I'm alive. There's not words in the dictionary to explain what the feeling is in my heart."

He was particularly pleased his entire family could be present, brothers, sisters, children and grandchildren. "I didn't dare say too much at the end, I'm on the emotional side. There are tears of sadness and tears of gladness and this was one of those times."

The head table included Daryle Ann Pickens, actress and daughter of Slim Pickens; five-time Canadian all-around cowboy Tom Bews; Cleve

Hill, long associated with the Lethbridge and District Exhibition, stock contractor Reg Kesler, author Herb Harker (Goldenrod), and trick roper Montie Montana.

MC Elton read telegrams and letters from Gene Autry, Montana Governor Ted Schwinden, Prime Minister Pierre Trudeau, Premier Peter Lougheed and entertainer Rex Allen.

A special presentation by Jim Shot Both Sides, former Chief of the Kainai Nation, was made to Herman and Agnes.

The Maine Anjou Association, Calgary Stampede, Canadian Professional Rodeo Cowboys Association, and long-time Calgary Stampede announcer Warren Cooper were among the unscheduled special presenters and speakers.

Cleve Hill dazzled those on hand with his wit. "Once I heard Herman talking about Maude, saying she had good eyes, carried her head high and had a good chest. I thought, you Lutheran son of a gun! Turned out he was talking about a mare at his own ranch. And when the Queen was in Calgary in 1951,

"Herman was in the Royal party and sat with Her Majesty. Herman helped tuck in a blanket behind her to keep her warm and gave her a little pat. Herman Linder is the only man, other than Prince Phillip, in Canada, the British Commonwealth or the world, who has patted the Queen's derriere – that's how important he is!"

MC Elton said: "Herman's the old story of the little acorn growing into a big tree – which proves you never know how far a nut is going to go."

Reg Kesler, rodeo stock contractor, friend and longtime working partner with Herman, said:

Herald Photo
This was the Lethbridge Herald's last Memorial to Harold on January 18th 2001

"The success of rodeo today is due to Herman Linder. Without him we'd have missed quite a part of rodeo in Canada and the United States."

At the end, Herman replied to his toasters: "The only thing I can think of to say is that I pray God forgives them for telling all those lies and at the same time I ask God to forgive me for believing them."

A few years later Herman Linder left us. A funeral service for Herman, the King of the Cowboys, was held in Cardston, with his passing January 18, 2001 at age 93. He will always be remembered as one of Canada's great rodeo legends. The LDS Church on the northern edge of Cardston was filled to capacity as his rodeo, ranching and other friends showed up to bid him adieu.

Senator Joyce Fairbairn of Lethbridge, a long-time friend, called it not just a privilege but a joy, to have had someone like Herman Linder involved in her life. "Herman was an important part of our country's history and culture," the Senator said. "He was a great part of our western culture.

"People like Herman, the Keslers and Mandevilles meant a lot in the settling and building of our rangelands, there's nothing like it anywhere else in Canada. These men were tough and brave, with an outstanding respect for the land.

"In Herman's life his relationship with people was important to him, not just rodeo and cattle people but all those around him like his neighbours, the Bloods. He was very proud of the fact he was a Kainai Chieftain. That's another special connection I had with him. It is sad to lose him."

Her father first introduced the Senator to

97

Herman when she was three years of age. He introduced him as the King of the Cowboys, something she has never forgotten.

Fairbairn said Herman Linder was just that, all through his life, calling his life a tremendous example of hard work, courage and generosity with a very strong commitment to the land.

"Herman was a great Canadian and one of my proudest moments, as a friend and as a Canadian, was to be with him and his daughter Rosemary in Ottawa when he received the Order of Canada. That was a real tribute to his life and it was a wonderful day. I've always felt of him as my little cowboy . . . I just loved the guy."

Harold Mandeville, another Canadian rodeo legend, began his career in 1946 and his first association with Herman came the same year. "I remember he had me drive his wife (Agnes) to the rodeo in Coleman for him," said Harold.

"After he quit riding he was producing rodeos with Harry Vold and Reg Kesler when they were together, and later just with Reg. Herman and Reg put on a lot of rodeos, including Expo '67. When I started rodeoing Herman was doing a lot of rodeos and we got along good. Herman was a businessman and he knew what he should and shouldn't do. He was a pretty descent person and he did a lot for rodeo." Harold recalled.

Mandeville's wife Pearl, a top barrel racer in her day, knew Herman as a businessman as well as a rodeo personality and often worked for him at his rodeo productions.

"Herman's daughter Rosemary and I always packed flags at Herman's rodeos and we timed events together as well," she said.

"We were hired by Herman as timers for the Montreal Expo rodeo. Herman was Mr. Personality, that's for sure. He certainly lived a good, long, interesting life and he never missed anything."

Besides daughter Rosemary (who is married to another Canadian rodeo champion, Tom Bews) Herman was survived by Adelaide, his second wife of 10 years, seven grandchildren and six great-grandchildren. Wife Agnes predeceased him in 1985, after 52 years of marriage, and son George in 1986 at age 43.

The Legendary Shelby Fight

As a life-long boxing fan I was more than pleased back in the late 1970s when, after year of trying, I finally made contact with James "Body" Johnson, the promoter of the Jack Dempsey - Tommy Gibbons heavyweight championship fight in Shelby, Montana in 1923. I had tried for years, and finally found him in Seattle, where we conducted an interview. A story first ran in The Herald in 1983, but was edited down to a mere handful of inches. I was crushed. Then, for the 80th anniversary of the fight in 2003, I re-worked the story and it ran in all its glory as part of the "Way We Were" series.

Then along came two wonderful additions. One the result of Alma Hanson's phone call - via her son - and another from an old tape recording of Orrin Turner's memories, passed on by his grandson Reed. Both stories added some other great personal touches to the battle, creating a first-hand look at the big 1923 event in Shelby.

In Shelby, Montana July 4 has a double meaning, though it must be admitted very few, if any today, were witness to the actual event.

Certainly no one remembers first-hand the signing of the U.S. Independence document in 1776, and you'd have to be at least 95 to even have any vivid memories of Shelby's only day in the international spotlight. It was July 4, 1923 when Jack Dempsey, the heavyweight boxing champion of the world defended his title in the little western railway town, against challenger Tommy Gibbons.

Yet, the story of the Dempsey-Gibbons fight lives on, and remains Shelby's major claim to fame nine decades later.

It was 1975 when I first made contact with the promoter of the infamous heavyweight battle and we conducted a telephone and mail – this is pre-email remember – correspondence. The reason for the initial contact was the death of

Dempsey, a man who fought in boxing's first million-dollar gate and was said to have toughened his hands and face by soaking them in brine. Sadly, James W. "Body" Johnson has now passed away, as has every other combatant, organizer, moneyman and person intricately involved in the historic bout.

At one time I owned an eight mm film of the fight - though it was not of high quality - but it showed it wasn't that great a contest.

Truth is, the fight itself was far over-shadowed by the pre-fight hoopla and the behind-the-scenes negotiations, threats and promises of men like Dempsey's manager Jack "Doc" Kearns and my promoter-acquaintance, who had long moved to Spokane when I first contacted him.

Body Johnson was 76 years of age in 1975 when we talked, and he laughed when he said the

Garry Allison Collection

The Great Jack Dempsey

99

fight was there in black and white - on film - for folks to see, but he was forever trying to set the record straight about the pre- and post-fight goings-on.

"Personally, I've been more interested in forgetting the whole affair than recounting it for the past (then) 50 years or so," he told me. "The actual fight itself was an accident to begin with and I never intended this fight would be held . . . and would not have done it had I thought I would get into the mess that we all did. So the answer is no, to your question - I would not do it all over again."

It was actually in 1920 when things started to take shape for Dempsey's trek to Shelby. In 1920 Dempsey disposed of Billy Miske and Bill Brennan, both in title bouts, setting the stage for boxing's first million-dollar gate with Dempsey and Frenchman George Carpentier in 1921.

The July fight in Shelby would be the next time Dempsey stepped into the ring, this time against Tommy Gibbons, a quick-handed, defensive fighter and brother of popular middleweight Mike Gibbons. Gibbons was initially offered $50,000 for his crack at the crown though he took home much less in the end.

Johnson, just 23 at the time, started along his road into boxing history by reading a newspaper article in the Great Falls Tribune in February, 1923. The article said Dempsey was being offered $100,000 to box in Montreal, and the idea came to Johnson to wire Dempsey's manager, Doc Kearns, and double that offer for a title bout in Shelby.

Johnson was in the real estate business at the time, with his father, James. A., a Canadian by birth. His father was one of the founders of Shelby and the

Johnson Photo Collection
The 1923 Dempsey-Gibson fight promoter James "Body" Johnson

town's first mayor. James A. had made his money in cattle and, sheep; he was also a storeowner, hotel owner and publisher of the Shelby Promoter for a while. He was the First State Bank president and involved in real estate when the fight idea came along. (James A. died in 1938.)

The idea behind it all was Johnson was looking for publicity in order to get real estate sales moving, back to the levels of the previous year when sales boomed, mainly due to the discovery of oil at Sunburst and Kevin, Montana.

At one time the booming little town of Shelby was known as The Tulsa of the West.

"Like my father, I wanted to help put Shelby on the map . . . that was what really got me into the fight game," Johnson later wrote in a short, documented history of the fight.

What started out as a publicity stunt, suddenly became quite real when Kearns accepted the offer. It came as a real surprise to Johnson who had not really even expected a reply, let alone approval. The negotiations themselves were epic in proportions. To shorten a long tale, the $200,000 original offer grew to $300,000 while Johnson was out of the picture for a while due to injuries sustained in a plane crash June 10.

During the time Johnson was out of the picture another $100,000 payment was negotiated with Kearns, at which time Kearns was to tell the press the fight was a certainty. Final arrangements called for a payment of $100,000 cash upon Kearns' signing for the fight, $100,000 to be paid by June 15 and the new, and final, $100,000 July 2, two days before the fight.

Johnson priced tickets at $50 for a ringside seat - this was in the era when a steak in a

U.S. Library of Congress Photo
Tommy Gibbons

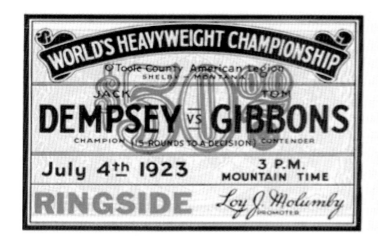

Shelby eatery would set you back 50 cents.

Among those to be seated at ringside were James A. and James W. Johnson and renowned western artist Charlie Russell.

With the signing, Shelby, headed by the Johnsons, set about to build a 40,000-seat arena to hold the thousands of fight fans expected to head west - and south from Alberta - to see the era's most popular sportsman battle Tommy Gibbons - who looked more like a professor than a fighter - for the greatest prize in sport, the heavy-weight boxing championship of the world.

It was a grand idea. A 40,200-seat outdoor wooden arena was to be built on the west side of Shelby, a town of a few thousand people, to attract the fight fans of the world.

It was July 4, 1923 and promoters expected to be turning away fight fans in the still fairly wild west as they flocked to this prairie town to see the great Jack Dempsey. It would be his fourth title defence.

The arena, including lumber, labour and all other costs set the promoters back $87,000 claimed the late "Body" Johnson, a key man behind the epic heavyweight tussle.

"It was built near convenient railroad siding locations for accommodation of special trains, on land furnished free by our real estate firm (James A. Johnson Company)," Johnson told me more than a decade before his death. "The Great Northern had built a large siding near the arena site. We had as many as 30 special trains at one time scheduled before the cancellations started pouring in.

"It was intended people coming in by special train would be sleeping and eating on the special railroad cars while they were in Shelby for the fight."

The lumbermen agreed to supply the lumber when the American Legion Post designated Body's father, James A., as treasurer of the fight association. The Toole County Legion Post 52 became involved because the Legion held the rights to promote fights within the state.

"It was agreed the Legion branch would receive $25,000 out of the first net of the proceeds. Problem was, there were no proceeds. From that time on, not only was my father the

40,000 seat arena built on the west side of Shelby, MT for the July 4, 1923 fight

treasurer, but he was an active general manager," Johnson stated about his father's involvement.

The arena was to be built of two-inch planking and larger timbers, lightly nailed together. The idea was for the structure to be demolished and sold to the oilfields for drilling rig construction after the fight.

"This is exactly what happened, but there was another part, the lumber companies' liens, which came into the picture with the showing of the fight films," said Johnson. "I was able to get a complete release for my father and I of all claims against us, personally, through the sale to them of motion picture rights for the states of Minnesota and Wisconsin."

Johnson said the story of the film was never completely told, except for small accounts he wrote. But he called the film rights saga as interesting as the fight itself.

"Don't forget, we were labouring under the famous Jack Johnson Law, a federal law which forbade the interstate transportation of any fight film of any professional fight within the boundaries of the United States or its possessions. Otherwise, we would never have lost any money on the fight. The films would have paid for it."

As for the 40,000 seats, created from 1.25 million board feet of lumber, well, 28,000 of them remained empty. There were 24 of the special trains cancelled due to newspaper reports of wild-eyed, gun-totin' cowboys and Indians and a need for Dempsey to have a heavy police guard for his march from his train 500 yards to the arena. Reality was, the only police on hand were the sheriff and the local officers and the wild-west scare never did materialize.

Of the 12,000 people in the stands - one outside estimate was double that number - a large portion came in through the 32 entrance ways free of charge when ticket sellers left their post just prior to the main event.

Johnson said the official paid attendance was 7,966. He also said in 1975 he still felt it was the negative press coverage that was really behind the

financial failure of the fight. It was brought on because Kearns failed to publicly state the fight was on, even a few days ahead of July 4.

Legend has it, despite the low gate, Dempsey was well paid for the fight, through pre-fight payments, and Gibbons fought for nothing. Johnson was quick to say Gibbons received $7,500 in advance of the bout, along with a free home for he and his family, with all expenses paid while he trained in Shelby. Gibbons was also able to collect daily fees from those who came to see him prepare for the great Dempsey.

Johnson said Eddie Kane, Gibbons' manager, would carry away a sack full of silver and folding money daily from the training camp. As well, thanks to the fight, Gibbons also received a 20-week vaudeville contract, beginning immediately after the fight, and he also signed a contract to fight Carpentier as a result of the Dempsey battle. The vaudeville contract kind of puts a dint in a story that Gibbons journeyed to Lethbridge after the fight to spend some time.

It was said by some Lethbridge people he had a bout with Lethbridge leather-tosser and dance hall owner, Dick Burgman, who had a dance hall on 13th Street North. The story is Burgman knocked out the man who just fought for the heavyweight title. It sure has a Ripley's Believe It Or Not twist to it, and you can believe it, or not, as you so choose. But I wouldn't bet money on it!

It is just another of the many stories that grew up around the Dempsey-Gibbons battle, the type of stories James "Body" Johnson spent his life trying to erase by telling, what he called, the Truth About '23.

Garry Allison Photo
Dick Burgman's fancy brick home still stands along 5ᵗʰ Avenue North

The main attraction - Jack Dempsey himself - received his cash, at least most of it. But Dempsey was probably the only one smiling after his July 4, 1923 championship fight in Shelby's 40,000 seat outdoor boxing stadium. After all, Dempsey won, and he did receive about $250,000 for his 15 rounds of work. Dempsey had received $100,000 up front to sign for the bout, and promoter "Body" Johnson - a nickname he had since being a

102

young boy - said Dempsey received his second $100,000 payment on schedule, just prior to the bout - after a great deal of behind-the-scenes carrying on.

Upon receiving his second payment Johnson said Dempsey's manager, "Doc" Kearns, was to make a public statement that the fight would be on for certain, no matter what. The idea behind the confirmation statement was to bring in special trainloads of fans and boost ticket sales. Problem was, Kearns never made the statement to the press, Johnson stated during our 1975 telephone interview.

However, an agreed upon final payment to the champion, to reach the promised $300,000, was never made, due to the intervention of the Internal Revenue folks. But it is said the ever-wiley Kearns did manage to carry off, in a little black bag, the $54,000 collected by ticket sellers at the gate, with the IRS' blessing. The IRS later filed a lien against Body Johnson and his father for taxes. It took years before the lien was finally settled.

"The federal tax lien for uncollected taxes was $100,000, which we settled at the end of several years for an offer in compromise of a cash payment of $100," said Johnson. "It is difficult to estimate the total money lost by people who invested in concessions, some in parking lots and things of that sort. But, as far an individuals were concerned, my father and I lost about $165,000 - a lot of money in those days - plus about five years of my time trying to recover from the federal tax liens, etc.

"One of the strangest pieces of irony in connection with the whole affair concerned our real estate business, J. Johnson and Co. The idea behind promoting the fight was to spark an interest in real estate sales in the community. From the time of the contract signing in Chicago to the end (and I mean the end) of our company that fall, we didn't sell one damn dollar's worth of real estate. Here I had started the whole thing for no other reason than to help sell real estate.

"I don't think anyone was 'hosed' - anything we did we did to ourselves. Of course, in the end it was Kearns who ultimately engineered the ridiculous arbitrary increase in Dempsey's purse from an agreed on $200,000 to $300,000. You know, Doc Kearns would not even let us talk to Dempsey. But I did have several talks with

Dempsey and his father at his training camp. Had he been free of Kearns, the promotion would likely have been a success."

As for the fight itself, Johnson, was pleased. He said it was a good fight, and he believed everyone else who saw it live, or saw the motion pictures of the bout, thought so as well.

"Don't forget Dempsey's answer to Kearns' question at the end of the fifth round," Johnson said. "Kearns asked: 'Why in the hell don't you go out there and knock the s.o.b. out?' Well, Dempsey replied: `How the hell can I knock him out if I can't hit him?'

"I personally was standing in Dempsey's corner at the moment this was spoken," Johnson emphasized. "In fact, Gibbons very nearly knocked Dempsey out during the fifth round and would have, probably, but he was a little bit afraid to follow through on one very well-landed right cross to Dempsey's chin. It caused Dempsey to drop his guard and sag back against the ropes. Gibbons told me over dinner at his house that night he just got too cautious after Dempsey almost knocked him out in the first round."

Body Johnson, who was born May 23, 1899, "with no one present to help my mother other than an Indian woman on the banks of the Marias River," moved away from Shelby a few years after the fight to make his home in Spokane.

"There are many reasons why I left Shelby, none of which had anything to do with the fight," he said. "I had been very active all my life, made a lot of money, and lost a lot of money. I had many enterprises, more successful ones than unsuccessful."

In later years he kind of lost interest in boxing, and by 1975 said he couldn't remember when he saw his last good live bout. He did think the fighters of the 1920s and 1930s would have murdered any of the men of the 1960s and 1970s however.

One of the last things Body Johnson said to me, was to encourage me to pass on the truth of the Shelby fight, an intriguing part of boxing history. He knew the story of the Shelby fight would continue to be told and retold, each time with an extra ingredient added, just like a good stew recipe that is passed on through generations. From what Johnson said and wrote, it seems to be a fact that truth is often stranger than fiction - but truth, spiced with a touch of fiction, always seems better in the story-teller's eye.

In 1966, Johnson did write a short booklet, *"The Truth About '23"* where he tells it like it was. In autographing the booklet, he wrote: "I trust the truth is of interest to a newsman." He also said, "the truth is really better than any of the imaginative accounts I have ever seen."

Alma Hansen proved to me just how wrong a supposition can be. I had hinted that very few people who witnessed the 15-round battle would still be alive, particularly if they were aged 20 or so when the fight occurred - after all that would make them 100 years of age.

Well, fact was, when she sat down with two of her girl friends to watch Dempsey win the decision over Gibbons, Alma (Coombs) Hansen was a 26-year-old schoolteacher from Cardston.

That's right, it meant this dynamic little lady was 105 years of age when she phoned me in 2003 - and she was almost as spry and as sharp as Dempsey was the day of the fight under the hot Montana sun.

"A couple of my girl friends, my father and a friend of his drove down to Shelby and camped out in two tents, on the outskirts of town. We girls were just there for an outing, not to see the boxing. It turned out to be a fun weekend and we stayed there two nights and two days."

Alma's best friend, Anne Steed (Green) also a teacher and the niece of Lethbridge sportsman Tom Green, and Norma Anderson (Bullock), a nurse, had jumped into Alma's father's car, (Mark A. Coombs). Along with a male friend of her father, S.O. Low of Cardston, they headed south. As Alma recalls it was an old Dodge which her father guided over the dirt and gravel road from Cardston to Shelby.

"I think it was a Dodge. My father had his first car in 1916, an old Model T, and this was just seven years after that first car. A few years after that fight my father bought a McLaughlin.

"We girls – none of us were married – had no interest in boxing, we just went for the ride. Also we went down for a girlfriend's wedding. There were a lot of activities too, with dances and such. There were dances all over the place and we went from one to another.

"There were a lot of things going on that weekend and the evenings were fun. We took most of our own food along. That was good because you couldn't eat anywhere, all the places were so full." Come the day of the fight the Cardston party drove to the new 40,000-seat wooden arena, the men going inside to watch the fight, the ladies staying in the car. They were having loads of fun just watching the people, coming past them by the hundreds and heading for the entrance gates.

"All of a sudden we heard a loud crash," she said. "Someone had crashed the gates. It was quite a loud sound and the people just swarmed in. They milled about and swept in, just like cattle milling through a gate on the range . . . I'm not very proud of this, even today, but we followed the crowds in. We wanted to see what was going on in there. Years later my husband was always embarrassed if I told people how we went in with no tickets.

"I don't know how they crashed it down, we were just sitting back a bit and watching the crowds. We hadn't planned on going in, not at all" Alma recalled.

Garry Allison Photo
Alma Hanson, at 105

The ladies thought the fight might last two or three rounds and they were content to sit in the car and wait for the men to come out. Then the gate came down and opportunity knocked. After all, these were three young women adventurous enough to drive on dirt roads in 1923 from Cardston to the oil town of Shelby. Even so, the ladies waited quite a while before venturing in.

"I couldn't believe it when we went in, just how many empty seats there were. As a result we got some really good seats in that big arena . . . I don't know if they were better than my father's

104

seats, I don't know where he sat.

We saw the whole thing, but oh, it was hot. It was a very hot afternoon, and we had no real interest in the fighters, though we had heard of them.

"After it started however, we got interested. We were kind of in favour of Dempsey, we had heard about him. I remember seeing Dempsey and thinking he was a good looking man. I later heard about some controversy around the fight, but I didn't know really what it was until I saw your stories in the Herald.

Alma ended with "I guess that fight put Shelby on the map. In later years when we'd just drive through Shelby I always liked to go back to the site where the arena was and remember back."

I was more than pleased to meet Alma and listen to her women's angle on the fight. She told me her husband used to chastize her years after for "getting in free," even though they didn't marry until many years later.

My Dempsey-Gibbons title fight story spawned yet another great tale. I was given a tape by Reed Turner of Raymond - a recording he did with his grandfather, James Orrin Turner - concerning an entirely different aspect of the heavyweight title fight weekend.

Orrin's stories centered on horses and touched briefly on Ray Knight and a rodeo he was putting on the same July 4 holiday that Dempsey and Gibbons were squaring off.

Orrin, born in 1900, lived most of his life south of Raymond along the Milk River Ridge. He had spent a lot of his youth working on the Kirkcaldy (Bar K2) Ranch, and also earned some extra money at times working in the Raymond Sugar Factory.

When word came of the big fight proposed for Shelby, Ray Knight decided he should put on a stampede in Shelby at the same time.

"Carpenters from Raymond went down and built a stampede arena, a great big one, in Shelby," Orrin said on the tape, recorded a short time before his passing in 1978.

Knight, Turner and a handful of select cowboys started out from the Kirkcaldy, moving across the fenceless countryside to Coutts with their horses and other rodeo provisions.

"We went down across the Milk River Ridge and I was driving an old chuckwagon we had at the ranch for years," said Orrin.

In Lethbridge, A.G. Baalim had control of the fight tickets, for all of western Canada. Seat sales opened in Lethbridge in mid-May. It was expected about 300 Lethbridge residents made the trip south for the fight. But if you didn't want to watch the fight, or go to the rodeo, you could stand out on main street and watch the action.

The cowboys had been around four or five days when Orrin took the lead team off his trail wagon, hooked them to another smaller wagon and drove them uptown for some groceries for the cook. He and another fellow went to the store and loaded the wagon up, heading back across the railroad track, down a slight slope.

"We came down the main street, and I had spooked the horses up a little, so everyone was looking at us, and those horses were really stepping up on the bits. I spanked them a little so they would look good. As we came down the hill and over the track it bounced the wagon a bit and the goose-neck slipped over the tongue. The wagon jumped ahead and hit the team in the rear end . . . and away they went down this busy street."

A train, in town for the big fight was at the crossing, but it had been split, so there was a line of cars on both sides of the railway track.

"As we came down that street, that team was a runnin'. Well, this fellow, hands in his pockets, had kind of walked out into the street and when he seen us commin' he just kinda froze."

Well, the wagon hit the guy dead centre, picking him up on the tongue right between the two running horses. And Orrin, try as he might, couldn't hold up the horses because every time he pulled back the wagon horses would hit the helpless pedestrian, just hanging on the front.

"This fellow was right on that tongue all the time, and he was just as white as a sheet. He was just petrified. He was so scared. I made a big circle with that wagon and came right back into the railroad crossing and headed for the train. I ran him right smack up to the train and the horses had to stop, they couldn't do nothing else.

Orrin continues "They stopped. The fellow was so scared he couldn't talk, he couldn't do nothing. And I wanted to laugh but I couldn't . . . I thought I could have killed him right there, but once we stopped it was funny.

"Well, he was so scared he just got loose off that tongue and walked off . . . I never did see or hear of him since. He had just froze to that tongue, with his hands still in his pockets. If he had gone down and that wagon gone over him it would have killed him right there."

The man had stepped off the curb with his hands in his pockets. As he turned towards the on-coming team, the wagon tongue went under his arm, between his elbow and side, locking his hand in his pocket and carrying him along on his exciting ride.

Little wonder, with all this excitement going on free in the streets, few fans were willing to pay $50 to see the Dempsey-Gibbons fight.

Body Johnson may have "made no proceeds" from the Shelby spectacle, but here we are, almost 100 years later still talking about the big event. As well as learning about the promoter's viewpoint, I was more than pleased to meet Alma Hanson and listen to her women's angle on the fight. She told me her husband chastized her for years after for "getting in free," even though they didn't marry until many years later.

And can't you just see Orrin Turner and his wagon team dashing down main street? Makes you wonder where Max Sennett and the Keystone Cops were at the time!

The Author - Garry Allison

Garry Allison served as Sports Editor of The Lethbridge Herald as well as District Editor, City Editor and at the end of his career in 2002, he was the Outdoors Editor. Garry moved into the Lethbridge Herald's sports department full-time in 1974, after spending 1957 to 1974 as a printer with The Herald.

An avid rodeo fan, Garry covered the sport - amateur, Native, college, high school and professional - throughout southern Alberta from the mid-1960s until his retirement in 2002. He also attended the first 10 Canadian Finals Rodeos as well as numerous Calgary Stampedes and North American Amateur championship rodeos in Denver, Colorado and EI Paso, Texas. Garry covered uncountable rodeos and even horse races on the Kainai and Piikani reserves.

Garry Allison

Garry earned Thomson Newspaper national and regional awards for editorial achievement, national awards and local awards for his extensive coverage of rodeo, high school sports and the outdoors. In 1979 he won the Max Bell Memorial Award for outstanding coverage of amateur sports in Alberta, and as a result is enshrined in the Alberta Sports Hall of Fame. As well he was inducted into the Lethbridge Sports Hall of Fame in May, 2003. He has received the Canadian Professional Rodeo Cowboys Association's Jimmy Brown award for rodeo coverage in Canada and has been honoured by Ducks Unlimited Canada, on the national and local level for his coverage. He has been honoured by the Alberta and Lethbridge Fish and Game Associations, as well as Trout Unlimited Canada's Lethbridge chapter. In non-sports fields the General Stewart Branch of the Royal Canadian Legion, Korea War Veterans Association, the Great Canadian Plains Railway Society and the town of Coalhurst have honoured him. In 1984 he was named Parent of the Year by Coalhurst High School.

He was given a special Blackfoot name, Eagle Wing, by the Piikani Nation through Head-Smashed-In Buffalo Jump Interpretive Centre in 1996. Garry is a member of the Headdress Society of the Kainai Nation and in 2000 was honoured by the National Aboriginal Day program at Fort Whoop-Up. In 2002 he received the Queen's Golden Jubilee Medal and in 2003 was the Honorary Parade Marshall of the Whoop-Up Days parade.

Since retiring in 2002, Garry has continued writing, first for the Rocky Mountain Turf Club and then publishing books: - a *History of North Lethbridge, My Side of Town* - published by the Lethbridge Historical Society in Nov, 2005; *The People of the Mines,* published by the No. 8 Mine Society in April, 2005; *The Prairie Boys, the story of southern Alberta War Veterans* published by the Historical Society in September, 2006; *A 100-Year History of the Lethbridge Exhibition*, published in 1999; and in 2005 he also completed a collection of biographies for the Exhibition dealing with the presidents, general managers and members of the Hall of Fame for the past 108 years, *The People of the Exhibition.* In 2010 his book, *My Country* was published by the Historical Society and is a look at the people of southern Alberta.

Garry was a 31-year member of the General Stewart Branch of the Royal Canadian Legion. In 2006 he served as chairman of the Rocky Mountain Turf Chuckwagon committee, after four years on the committee. In 2007 he was elected to the Board of Directors for the Lethbridge and District Exhibition.

Garry and wife Mary have been married 50 years and have seven children and 21 grandchildren. They have also been Foster parents for more than 33 years, serving more than 78 children, and still have a boy in their home.

DATE DUE